EASY GUITAR
WITH NOTES & TAB

PRAISE AND WORSHIP

FOR GUITAR

ISBN 0-634-00226-0

HAL•LEONARD®
CORPORATION

7777 W. BLUEMOUND RD. P.O. BOX 13819 MILWAUKEE, WI 53213

Visit Hal Leonard Online at
www.halleonard.com

STRUM AND PICK PATTERNS

This chart contains the suggested strum and pick patterns that are referred to by number at the beginning of each song in this book. The symbols ⊓ and ∨ in the strum patterns refer to down and up strokes, respectively. The letters in the pick patterns indicate which right-hand fingers plays which strings.

p = thumb
i = index finger
m = middle finger
a = ring finger

For example; Pick Pattern 2
is played: thumb - index - middle - ring

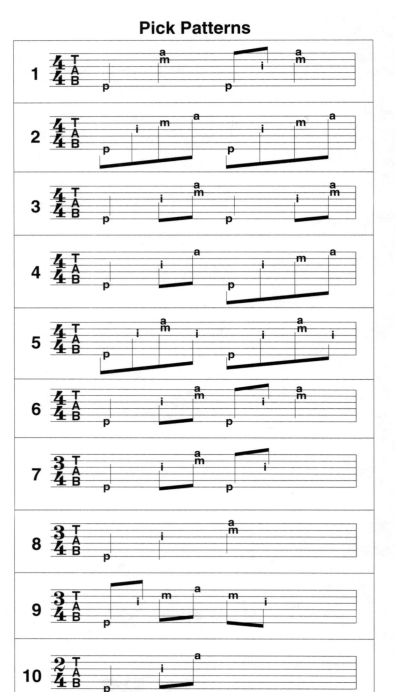

You can use the 3/4 Strum or Pick Patterns in songs written in compound meter (6/8, 9/8, 12/8, etc.).
For example, you can accompany a song in 6/8 by playing the 3/4 pattern twice in each measure.
The 4/4 Strum and Pick Patterns can be used for songs written in cut time (¢) by doubling the note time values in the patterns. Each pattern would therefore last two measures in cut time.

PRAISE AND WORSHIP

FOR GUITAR

All Hail King Jesus

Words and Music by Dave Moody

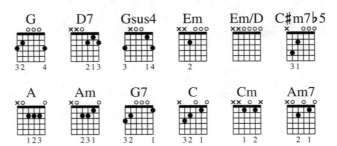

Strum Pattern: 4
Pick Pattern: 4

Moderately Slow

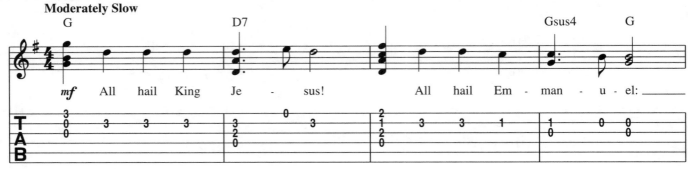

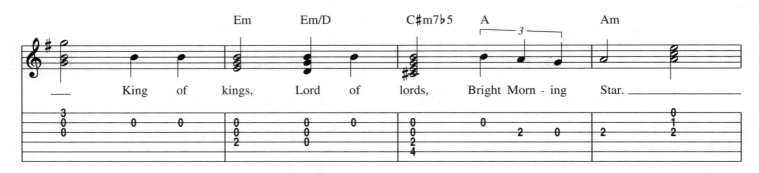

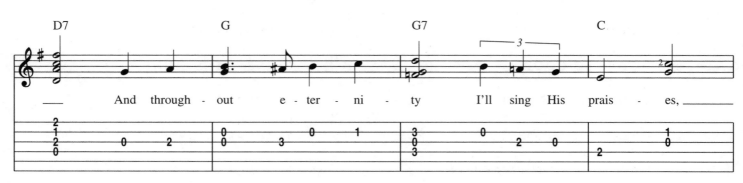

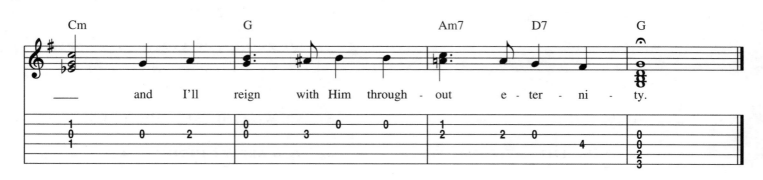

Amazing Grace

Words by John Newton
Traditional American Melody

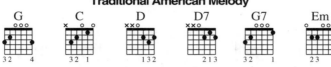

Strum Pattern: 7
Pick Pattern: 7

Additional Lyrics

2. 'Twas grace that taught my heart to fear,
   And grace my fears relieved.
   How precious did that grace appear
   The hour I first believed.

3. Through many dangers, toils and snares,
   I have already come.
   'Tis grace has brought me safe thus far,
   And grace will lead me home.

4. The Lord has promised good to me,
   His word my hope secures.
   He will my shield and portion be
   As long as life endures.

5. And when this flesh and heart shall fail,
   And mortal life shall cease.
   I shall possess within the veil
   A life of joy and peace.

6. When we've been there ten thousand years,
   Bright shining as the sun.
   We've no less days to sing God's praise
   Than when we first begun.

All Your Anxiety

Traditional

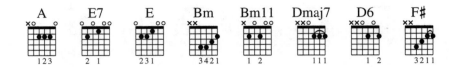

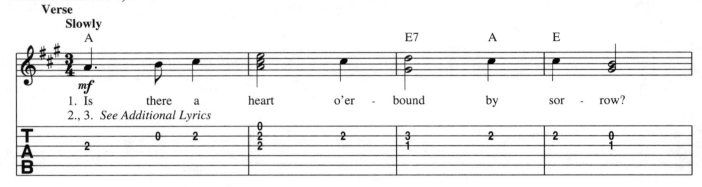

Strum Pattern: 7, 9
Pick Pattern: 7, 9

Verse
Slowly

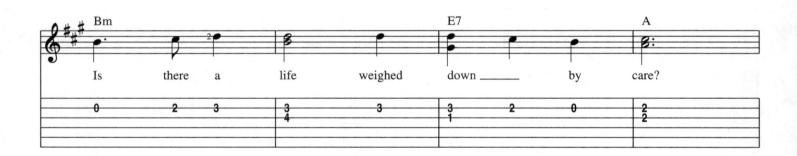

1. Is there a heart o'er - bound by sor - row?
2., 3. *See Additional Lyrics*

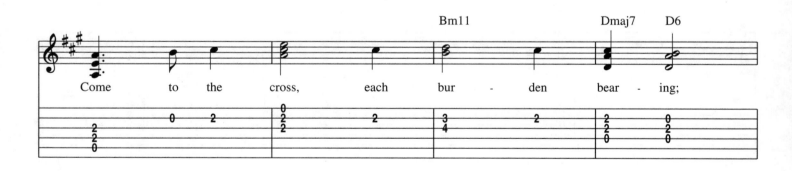

Is there a life weighed down _____ by care?

Come to the cross, each bur - den bear - ing;

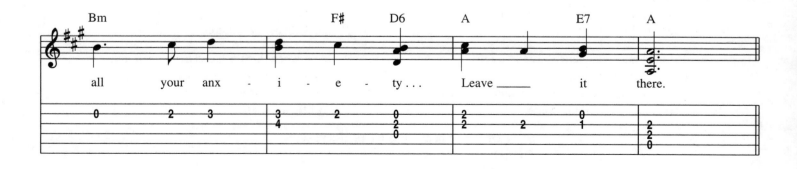

all your anx - i - e - ty... Leave _____ it there.

Chorus

All your anx - i - e - ty, all your care,

bring to the mer - cy seat... Leave it there.

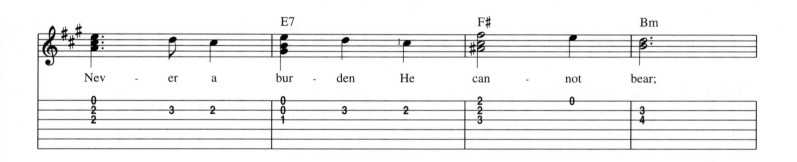

Nev - er a bur - den He can - not bear;

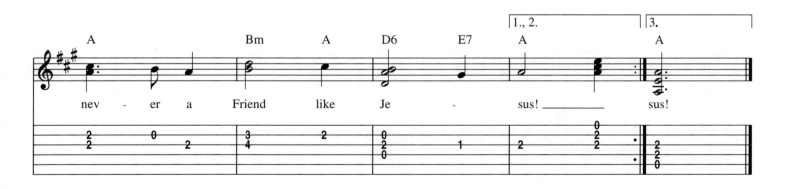

nev - er a Friend like Je - sus! _____ sus!

Additional Lyrics

2. No other friend so swift to help you;
No other friend so quick to hear.
No other place to leave your burden;
No other one to hear your prayer.

3. Come then at once; delay no longer!
Heed His entreaty kind and sweet.
You need not fear a disappointment;
You shall find peace at the mercy seat.

As the Deer

Words and Music by Martin Nystrom

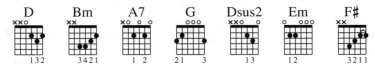

Strum Pattern: 1, 3
Pick Pattern: 2, 4

Verse
Moderately Slow

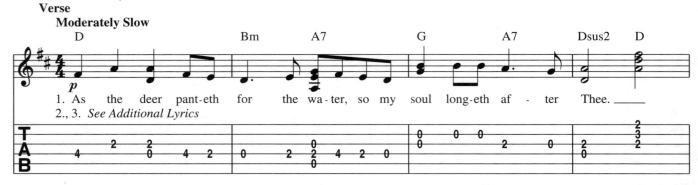

1. As the deer pant-eth for the wa-ter, so my soul long-eth af-ter Thee. ____
2., 3. *See Additional Lyrics*

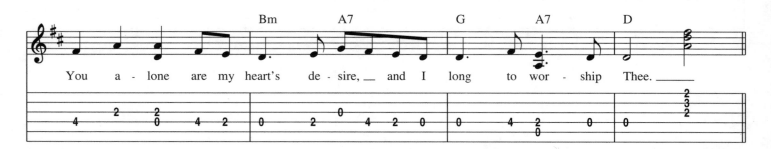

You a-lone are my heart's de-sire, __ and I long to wor-ship Thee. ____

Chorus

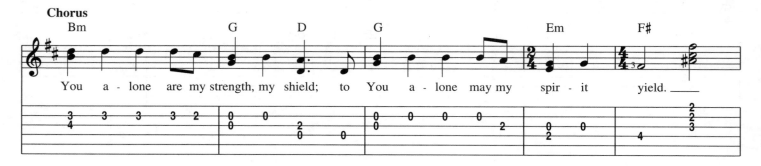

You a-lone are my strength, my shield; to You a-lone may my spir-it yield. ____

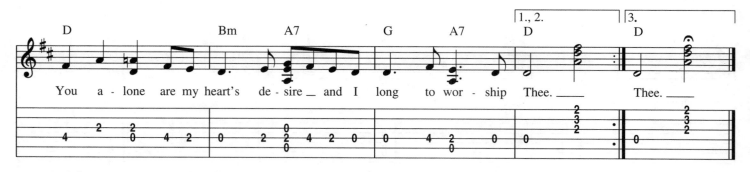

You a-lone are my heart's de-sire __ and I long to wor-ship Thee. ____ Thee. ____

Additional Lyrics

2. You're my friend and You are my brother,
Even though You are a King;
I love You more than any other,
So much more than anything.

3. I want You more than gold or silver,
Only You can satisfy;
You alone are the real joy-giver
And the apple of my eye.

Be Still and Know

Text from Psalm 46:10a, Exodus 15:26b
Traditional Music

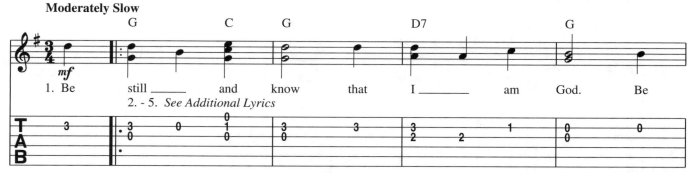

Strum Pattern: 7, 8
Pick Pattern: 7, 8

Verse
Moderately Slow

1. Be still _____ and know that I _____ am God. Be

2. - 5. *See Additional Lyrics*

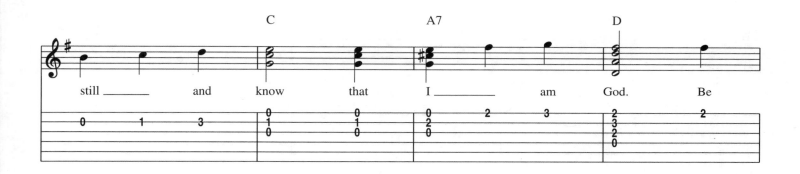

still _____ and know that I _____ am God. Be

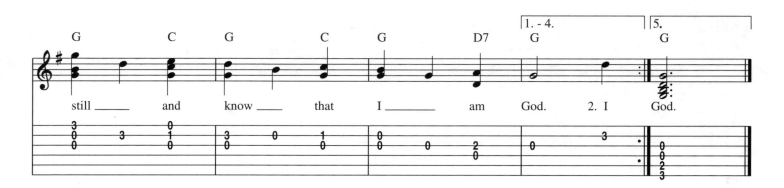

still _____ and know _____ that I _____ am God. 2. I God.

Additional Lyrics

2. I am the Lord that healeth thee.
I am the Lord that healeth thee.
I am the Lord that healeth thee.

3. My boundless mercy shall endure.
My boundless mercy shall endure.
My boundless mercy shall endure.

4. I love You with a steadfast love.
I love You with a steadfast love.
I love You with a steadfast love.

5. In Thee, O Lord, I put my trust.
In Thee, O Lord, I put my trust.
In Thee, O Lord, I put my trust.

Be Not Afraid

Traditional

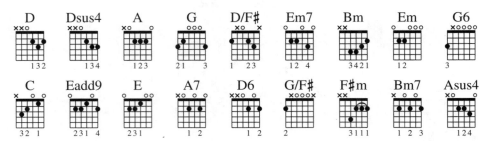

Strum Pattern: 4
Pick Pattern: 5

Verse
Moderately Slow

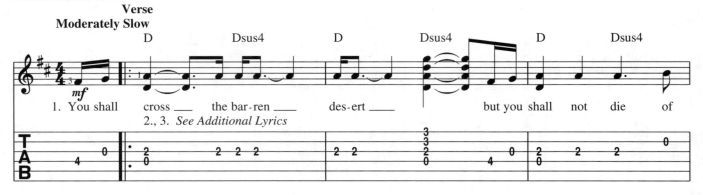

1. You shall cross the bar-ren des-ert but you shall not die of
2., 3. *See Additional Lyrics*

thirst. You shall wan-der far in safe-ty though you

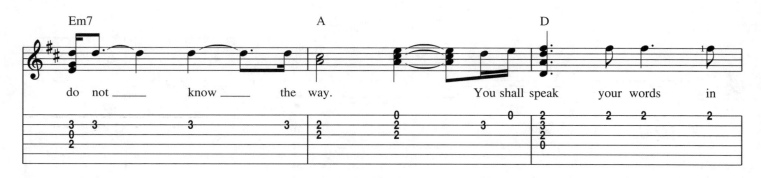

do not know the way. You shall speak your words in

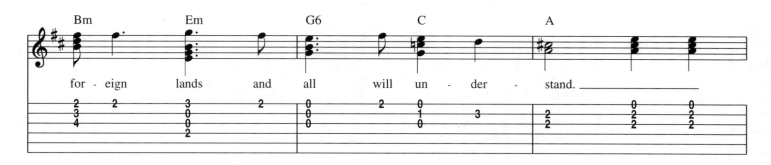

for-eign lands and all will un-der-stand.

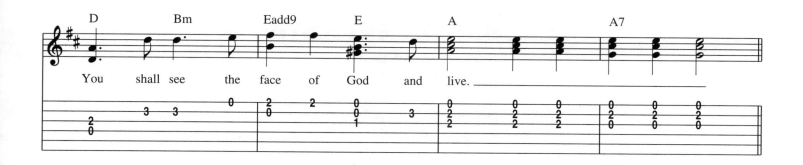

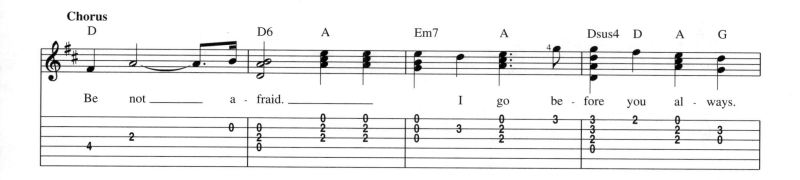

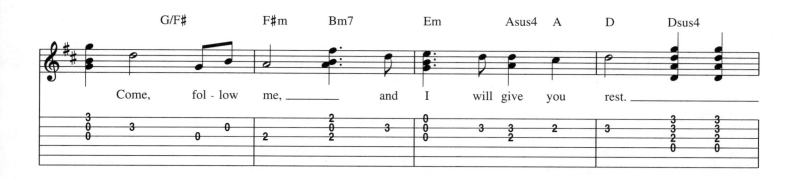

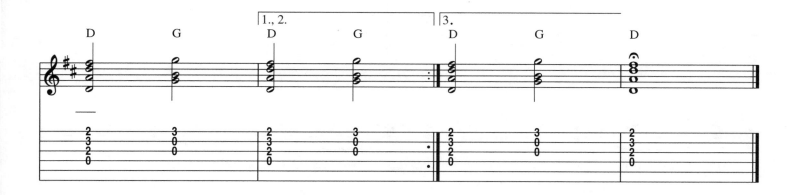

Additional Lyrics

2. If you pass through raging waters in the sea, you shall not drown.
   If you walk amid the burning flames, you shall not be harmed.
   If you stand before the pow'r of hell and death is at your side,
   Know that I am with you through it all.

3. Blessed are your poor, for the kingdom shall be theirs.
   Blest are you that weep and mourn, for one day you shall laugh.
   And if wicked tongues insult and hate you all because of me,
   Blessed, blessed are you!

Blessed Redeemer

Words by Avis B. Christiansen
Music by Harry Dixon Loes

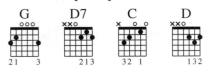

Strum Pattern: 8
Pick Pattern: 8

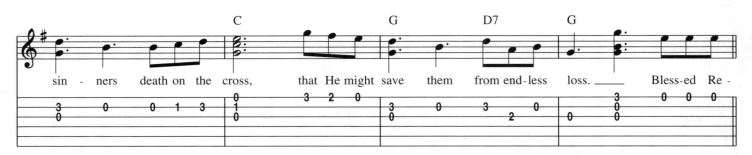

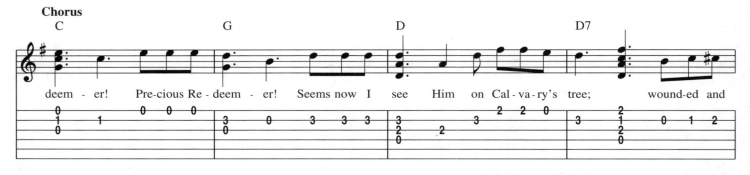

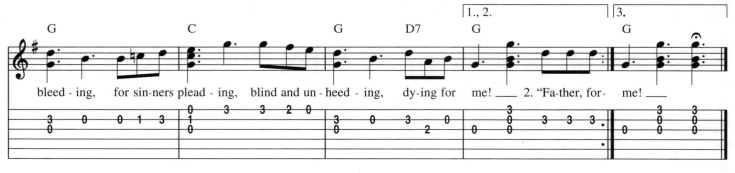

Additional Lyrics

2. "Father, forgive them," thus did He pray,
E'en while His life-blood flowed fast away.
Praying for sinners while in such woe,
No one but Jesus ever loved so!

3. Oh, how I love Him, Savior and Friend!
How can my praises ever find end?
Through years unnumbered on heaven's shore,
My tongue shall praise Him forevermore.

Come Christians Join to Sing

Words by Christian Henry Bateman
Traditional Melody

Strum Pattern: 1, 3
Pick Pattern: 2, 4

Verse
Moderately

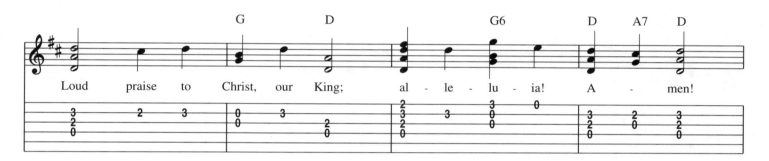

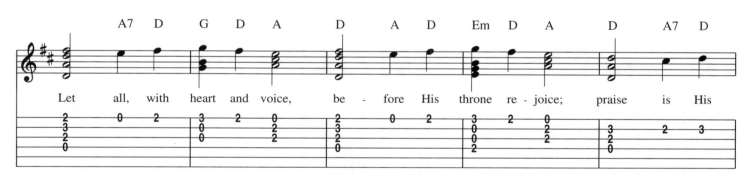

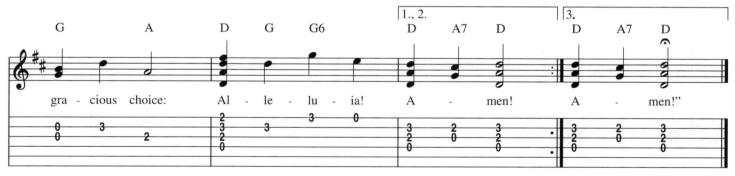

Additional Lyrics

2. Come, lift your hearts on high: Alleluia! Amen!
   Let praises fill the sky; alleluia! Amen!
   He is our Guide and Friend; to us He'll condescend;
   His love shall never end: Alleluia! Amen!

3. Praise yet our Christ again, alleluia! Amen!
   Life shall not end the strain; alleluia! Amen!
   On heaven's blissful shore His goodness we'll adore,
   Singing forevermore, "Alleluia! Amen!"

Blest Be the Lord

Words and Music by Dan Schutte

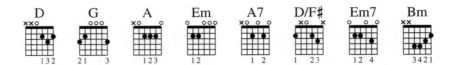

Strum Pattern: 3, 4
Pick Pattern: 4, 5

Chorus
Moderately

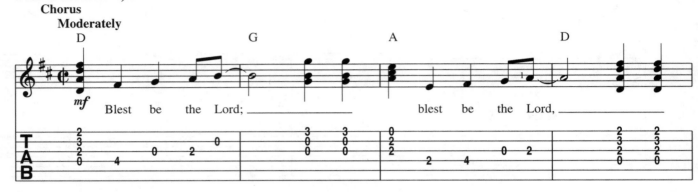

Blest be the Lord; _____ blest be the Lord, _____

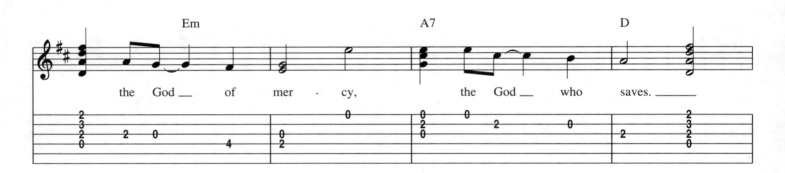

the God __ of mer - cy, the God __ who saves. _____

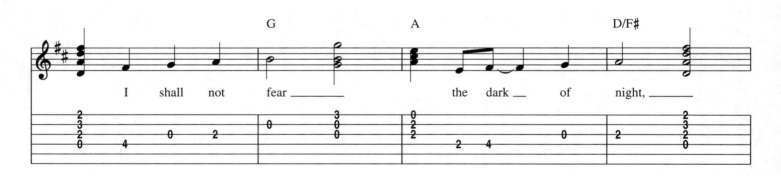

I shall not fear _____ the dark __ of night, _____

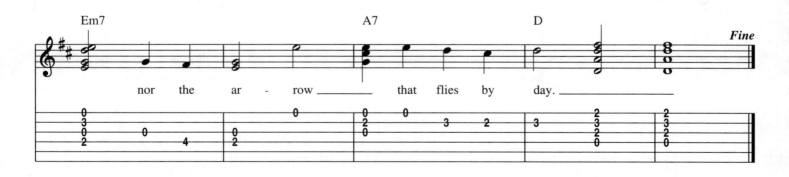

nor the ar - row _____ that flies by day. _____

Verse

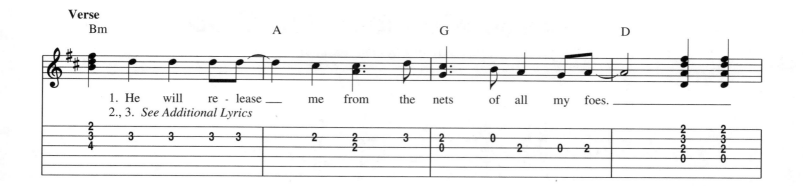

1. He will re - lease ___ me from the nets of all my foes. _____

2., 3. *See Additional Lyrics*

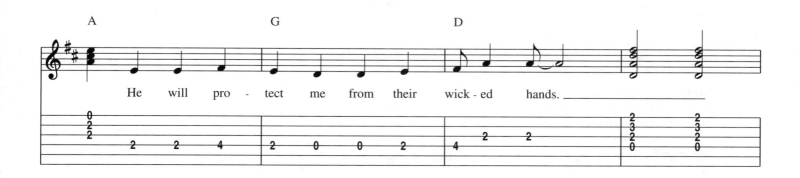

He will pro - tect me from their wick - ed hands. _____

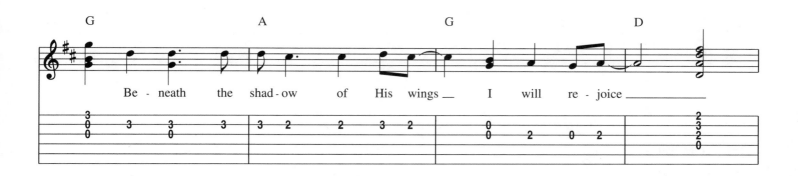

Be - neath the shad - ow of His wings ___ I will re - joice _____

D.C. al Fine

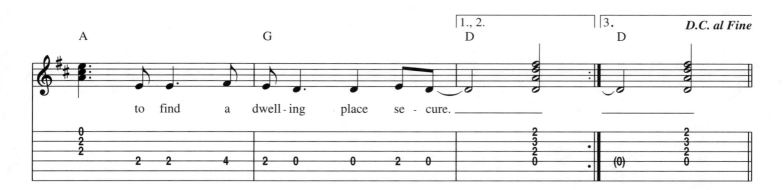

to find a dwell - ing place se - cure. _____ _____

Additional Lyrics

2. I need not shrink before the terrors of the night,
   Nor stand alone before the light of day.
   No harm shall come to me, no arrow strike me down,
   No evil settle in my soul.

3. Although a thousand strong have fallen at my side,
   I'll not be shaken with the Lord at hand.
   His faithful love is all the armor that I need
   To wage my battle with the foe.

Change My Heart Oh God

Words and Music by Eddie Espinosa

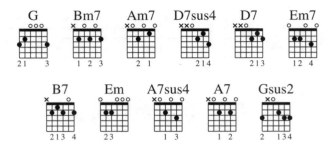

Strum Pattern: 4
Pick Pattern: 5

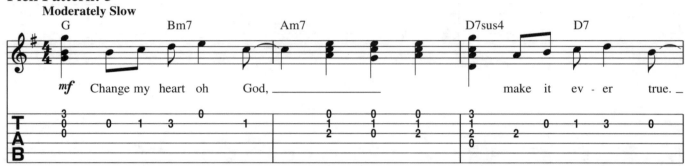

Change my heart oh God, _____ make it ev - er true. _

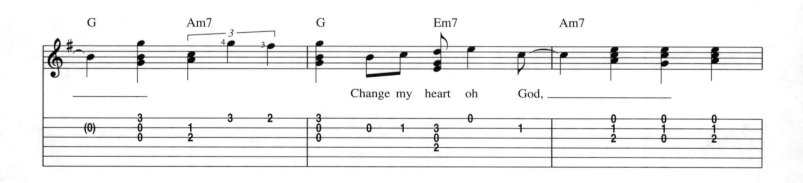

_____ Change my heart oh God, _____

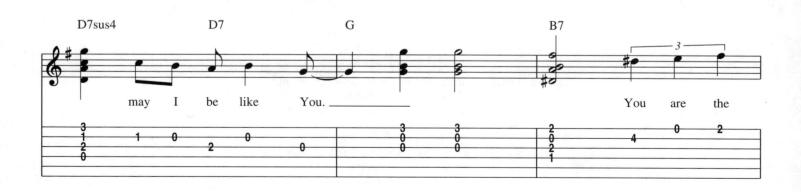

may I be like You. _____ You are the

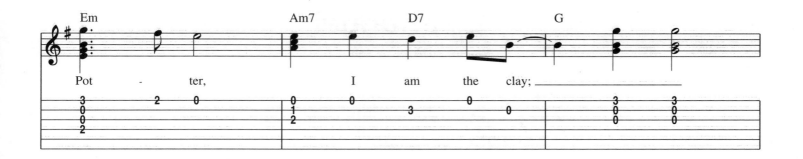

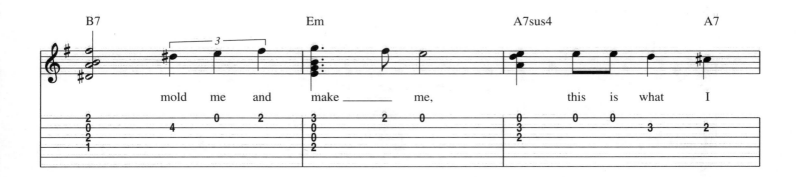

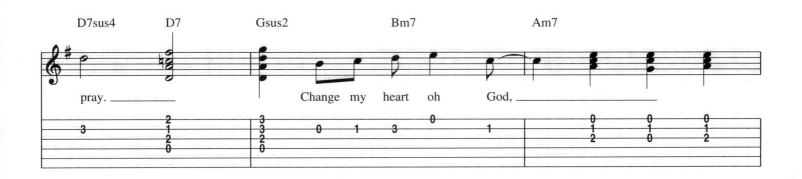

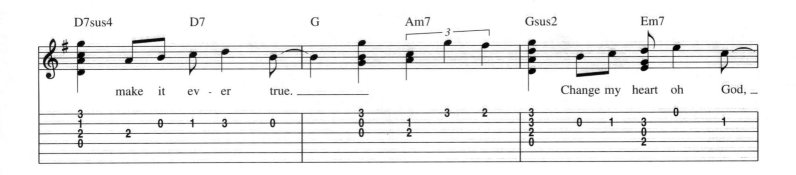

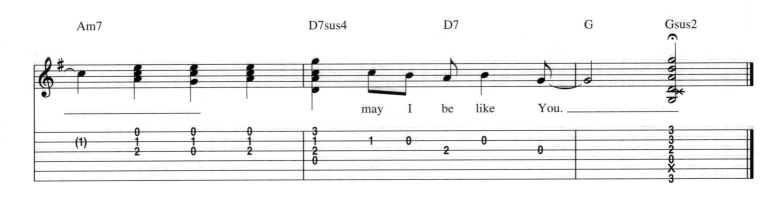

Emmanuel

Words and Music by Bob McGee

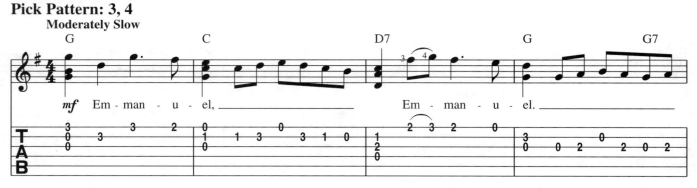

Strum Pattern: 2, 4
Pick Pattern: 3, 4

Moderately Slow

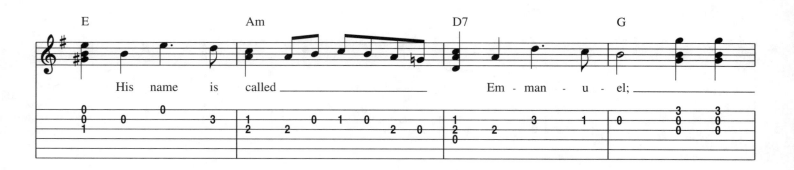

Em - man - u - el, _____ Em - man - u - el. _____

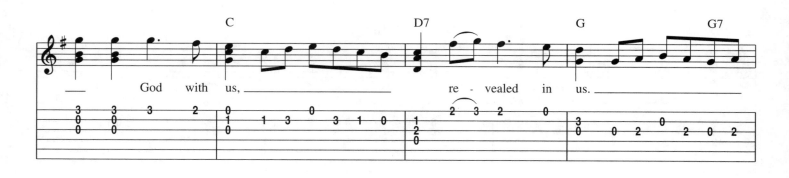

His name is called _____ Em - man - u - el; _____

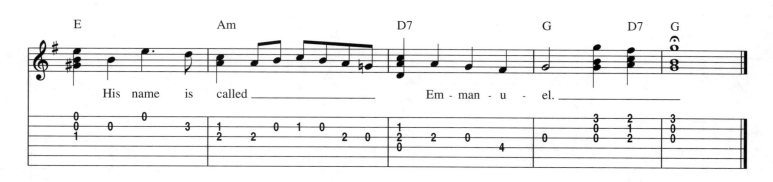

_____ God with us, _____ re - vealed in us. _____

His name is called _____ Em - man - u - el. _____

Glorify Thy Name

Words and Music by Donna Adkins

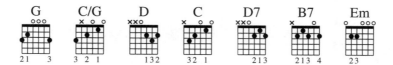

Strum Pattern: 1, 3
Pick Pattern: 2, 4

Verse
Moderately Slow

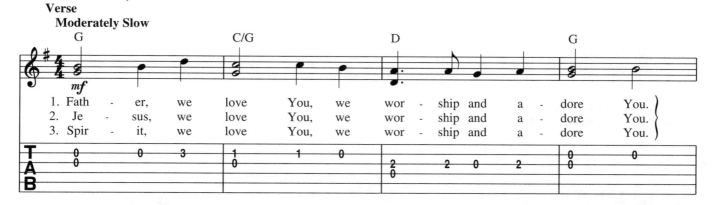

1. Fath - er, we love You, we wor - ship and a - dore You.
2. Je - sus, we love You, we wor - ship and a - dore You.
3. Spir - it, we love You, we wor - ship and a - dore You.

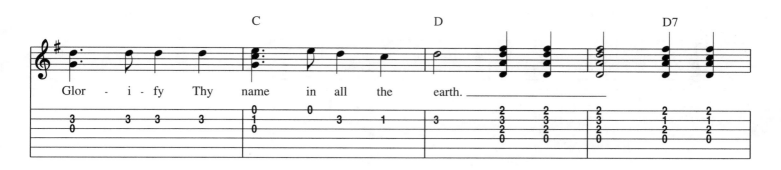

Glor - i - fy Thy name in all the earth. _____

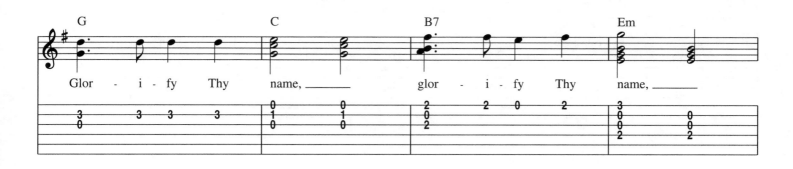

Glor - i - fy Thy name, _____ glor - i - fy Thy name, _____

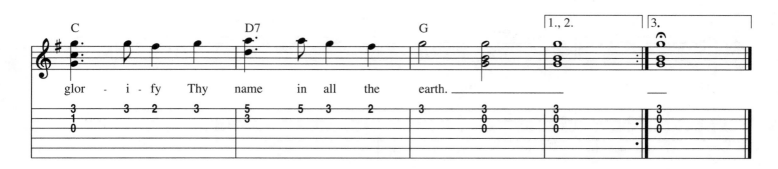

glor - i - fy Thy name in all the earth. _____

Give Thanks

Words and Music by Henry Smith

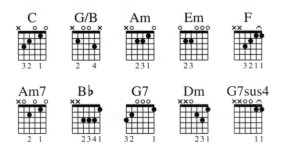

Strum Pattern: 1, 6
Pick Pattern: 2, 4

𝄋 **Verse**
Moderately Slow

1. Give (2.) thanks with a grate-ful heart; _ give thanks to the Ho - ly One. _ Give

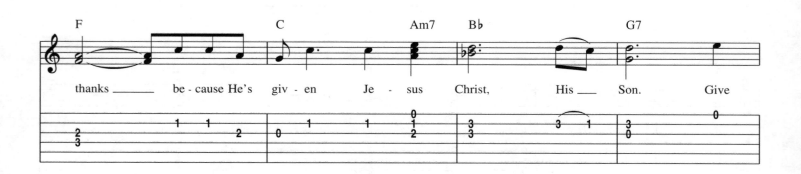

thanks _____ be - cause He's giv - en Je - sus Christ, His ___ Son. Give

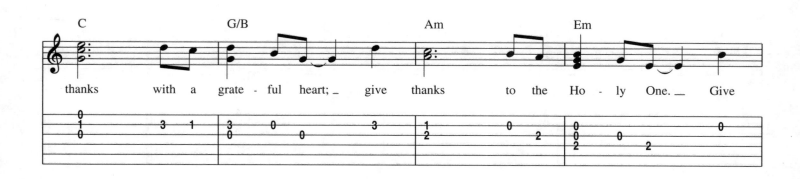

thanks with a grate - ful heart; _ give thanks to the Ho - ly One. _ Give

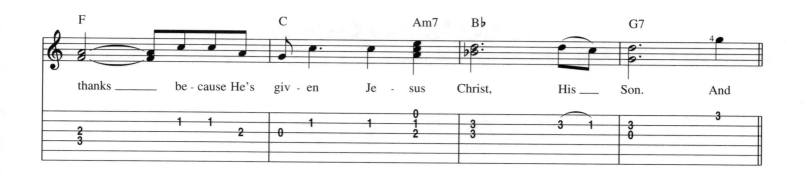

thanks _____ be-cause He's giv-en Je-sus Christ, His ___ Son. And

Chorus

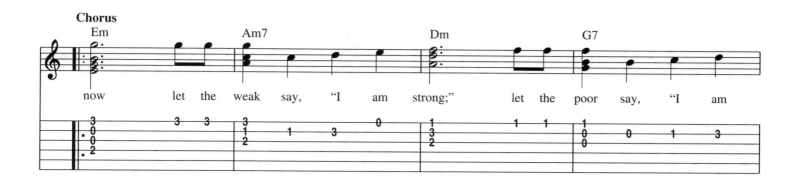

now let the weak say, "I am strong;" let the poor say, "I am

4th time, To Coda ⊕

D.S. al Coda
(take repeat)

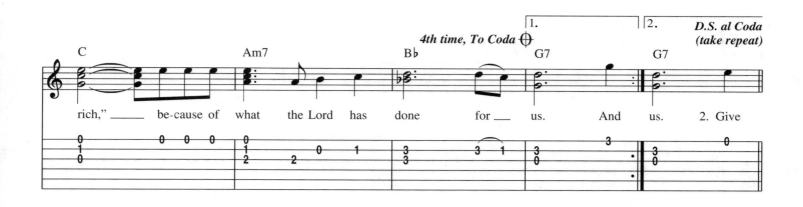

rich," _____ be-cause of what the Lord has done for ___ us. And us. 2. Give

⊕ *Coda*

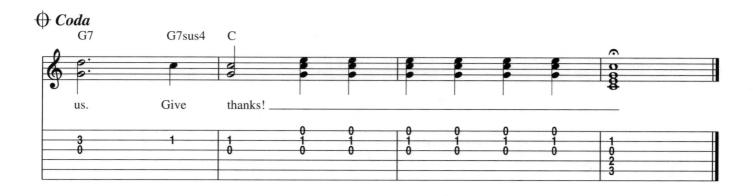

us. Give thanks! _____

God Is So Good

Traditional

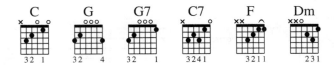

Strum Pattern: 2, 3
Pick Pattern: 2, 4

Verse
Moderately

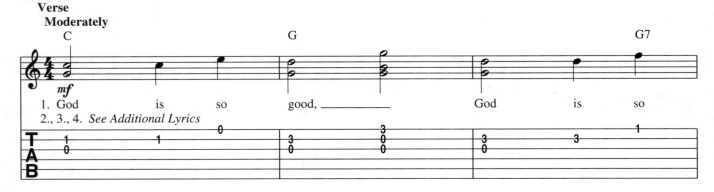

1. God is so good, _____ God is so

2., 3., 4. *See Additional Lyrics*

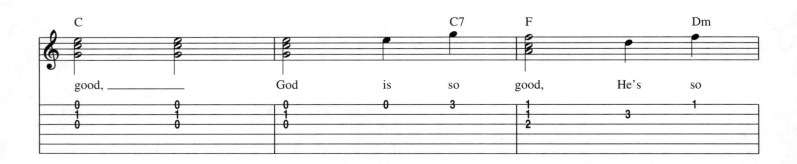

good, _____ God is so good, He's so

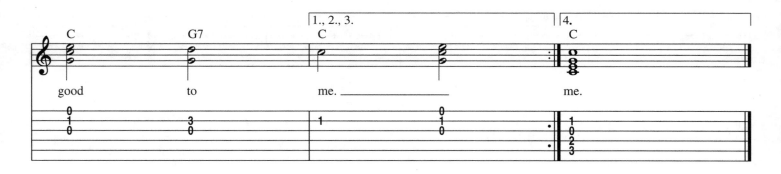

good to me. _____ me.

Additional Lyrics

2. He cares for me, He cares for me,
   He cares for me, He's so good to me.

3. He loves me so, He loves me so,
   He loves me so, He's so good to me.

4. God is so good, God is so good,
   God is so good, He's so good to me.

God of Grace and God of Glory

Text by Harry Emerson Fosdick
Music by John Hughes

Strum Pattern: 2
Pick Pattern: 2

Additional Lyrics

2. Lo! The hosts of evil round us
Scorn Thy Christ, assail His ways!
From the fears that long have bound us,
Free our hearts to faith and praise.
Grant us wisdom, grant us courage,
For the living of these days,
For the living of these days.

3. Cure Thy children's warring madness,
Bend our pride to Thy control.
Shame our wanton, selfish gladness,
Rich in things and poor in soul.
Grant us wisdom, grant us courage,
Lest we miss Thy Kingdom's goal,
Lest we miss Thy Kingdom's goal.

4. Set our feet on lofty places,
Gird our lives that they may be
Armored with all Christ–like graces
In the fight to set men free.
Grant us wisdom, grant us courage,
That we fail not man nor Thee,
That we fail not man nor Thee.

Have Thine Own Way Lord

Words by Adelaide Pollard
Music by George Stebbins

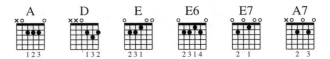

Strum Pattern: 8
Pick Pattern: 8

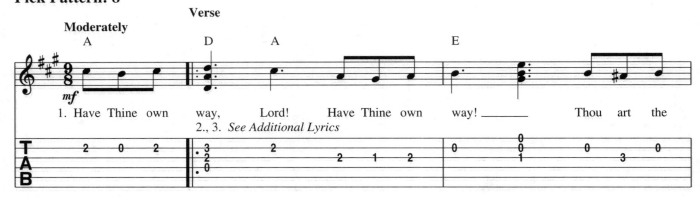

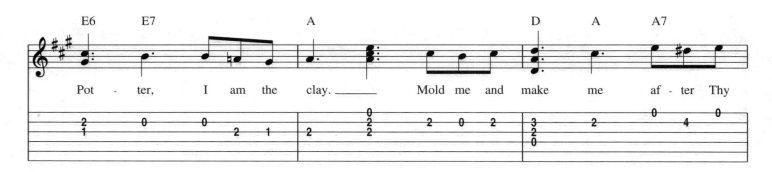

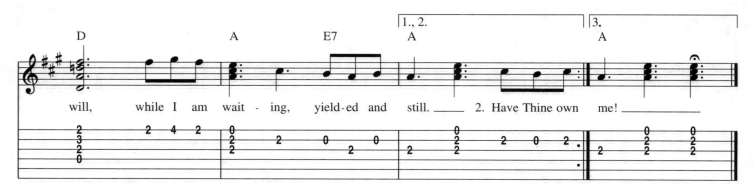

Additional Lyrics

2. Have Thine own way, Lord! Have Thine own way!
   Search me and try me, Master, today!
   Whiter than snow, Lord, wash me just now,
   As in Thy presence humbly I bow.

3. Have Thine own way, Lord! Have Thine own way!
   Hold o'er my being absolute sway!
   Fill with Thy spirit till all shall see
   Christ only, always, living in me!

He Is Lord

**Words and Music by Tom Fettke, Claire Cloninger
and Linda Lee Johnson**

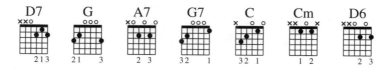

Strum Pattern: 1, 3
Pick Pattern: 2, 4

Verse
Moderately Slow

1. He is (2.) Lord, _____ He is Lord! _____ He is ris - en from the dead and He is

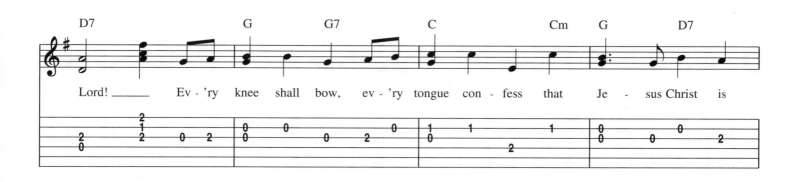

Lord! _____ Ev - 'ry knee shall bow, ev - 'ry tongue con - fess that Je - sus Christ is

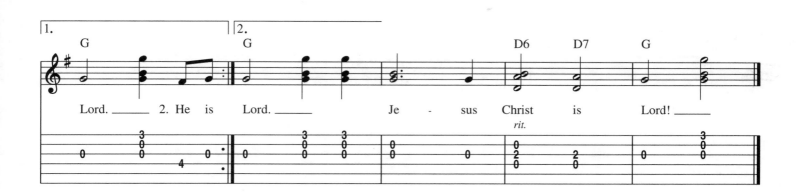

Lord. _____ 2. He is Lord. _____ Je - sus Christ is Lord! _____

Great Is the Lord

Words and Music by Michael W. Smith and Deborah D. Smith

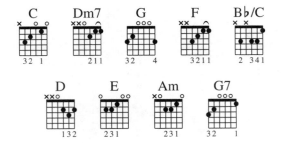

Strum Pattern: 8, 9
Pick Pattern: 8, 9

1., 2. Great is the Lord, He is ho - ly and just; by His pow - er we trust in His love. _____

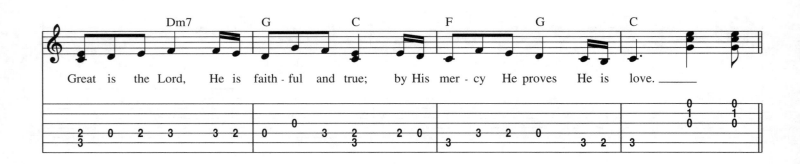

Great is the Lord, He is faith - ful and true; by His mer - cy He proves He is love. _____

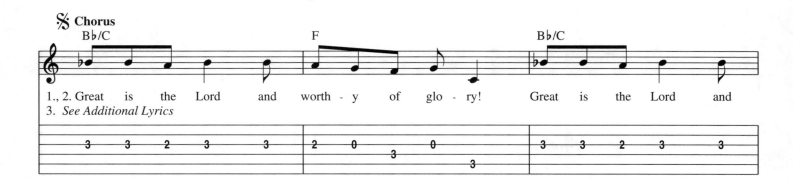

1., 2. Great is the Lord and worth - y of glo - ry! Great is the Lord and
3. *See Additional Lyrics*

worth - y of praise! Great is the Lord! Now lift up your voice, now

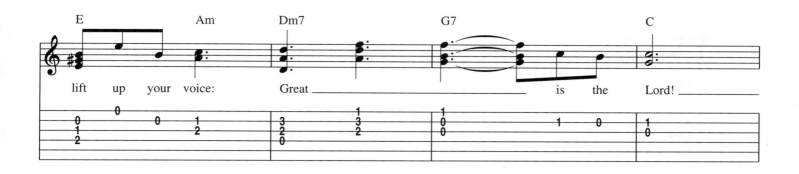

lift up your voice: Great _____ is the Lord! _____

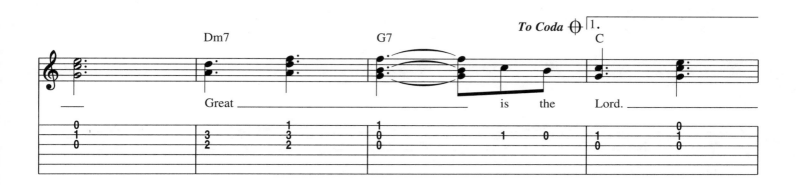

_____ Great _____ is the Lord. _____

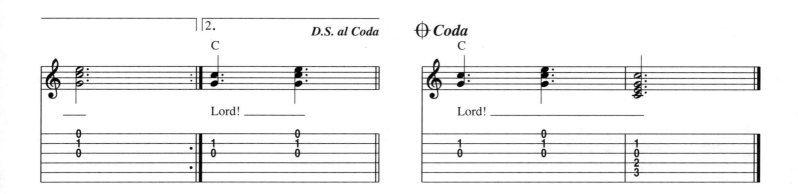

_____ Lord! _____   Lord! _____

Additional Lyrics

Chorus 3. Great are You, Lord, and worthy of glory!
Great are You, Lord, and worthy of praise!
Great are You, Lord! I lift up my voice,
I lift up my voice:
Great are You, Lord!
Great are You, Lord!

He Is Exalted

Words and Music by Twila Paris

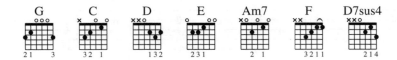

Strum Pattern: 8
Pick Pattern: 8

Lively

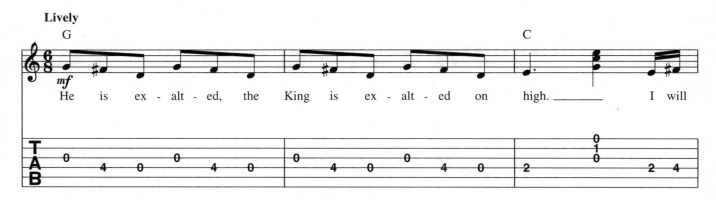

He is ex - alt - ed, the King is ex - alt - ed on high. _____ I will

praise Him. He is ex - alt - ed, for - ev - er ex - alt - ed and

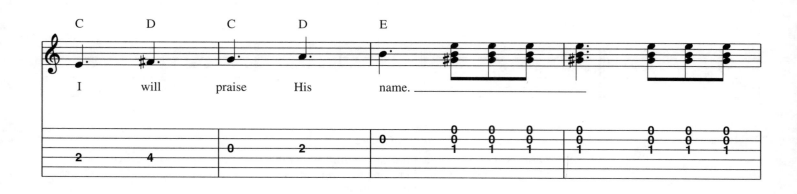

I will praise His name. _____

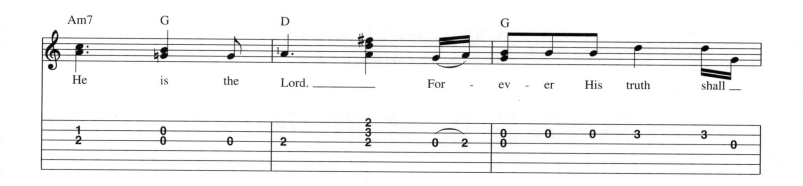

He is the Lord. _____ For - ev - er His truth shall __

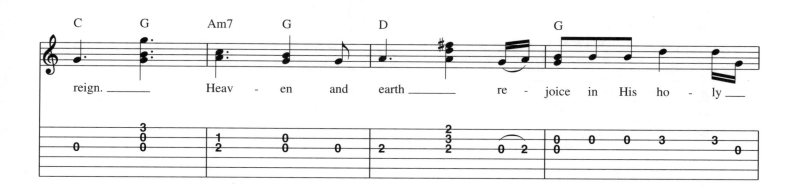

reign. _____ Heav - en and earth _____ re - joice in His ho - ly __

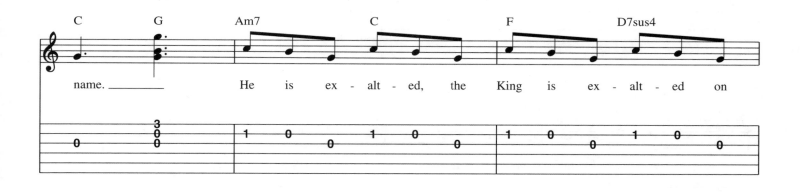

name. _____ He is ex - alt - ed, the King is ex - alt - ed on

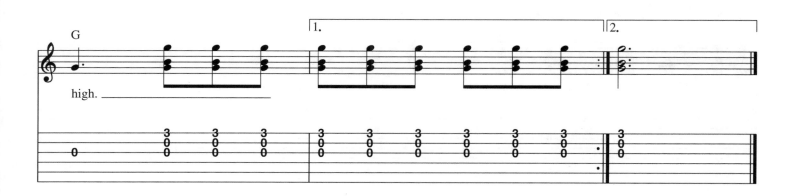

high. _____

Here I Am, Lord

Words and Music by Daniel L. Schutte

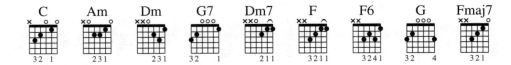

Strum Pattern: 2, 4
Pick Pattern: 1, 4

Verse
Moderately Slow

1. I, the Lord of sea and sky, I have heard My peo - ple cry.
2., 3. *See Additional Lyrics*

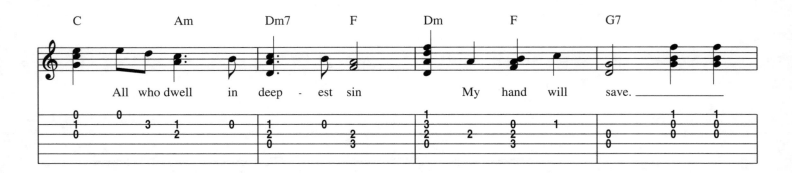

All who dwell in deep - est sin My hand will save. _____

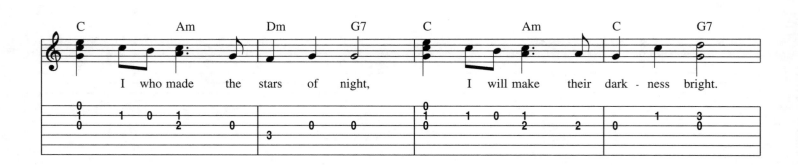

I who made the stars of night, I will make their dark - ness bright.

Who will bear My light to them? Whom shall I send? Here I

Chorus

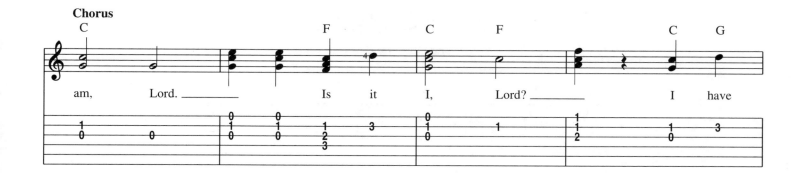

am, Lord. _____ Is it I, Lord? _____ I have

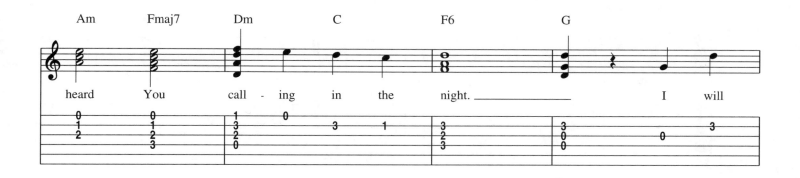

heard You call - ing in the night. _____ I will

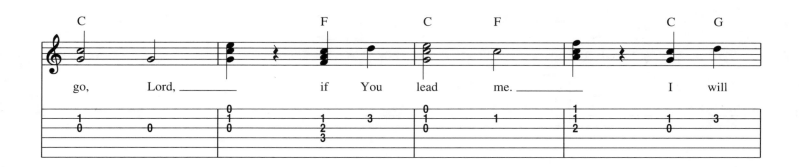

go, Lord, _____ if You lead me. _____ I will

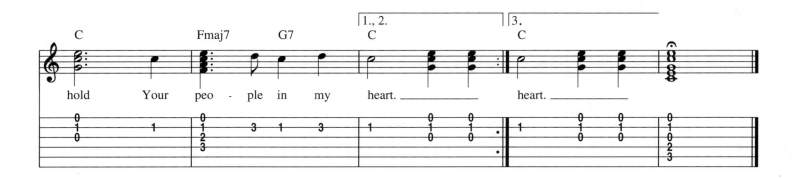

hold Your peo - ple in my heart. _____ heart. _____

Additional Lyrics

2. I, the Lord of snow and rain,
   I have borne My people's pain.
   I have wept for love of them,
   They turn away.
   I will break their hearts of stone,
   Give them hearts for love alone.
   I will speak My word to them.
   Whom shall I send?

3. I, the Lord of wind and flame,
   I will tend the poor and lame.
   I will set a feast for them,
   My hand will save.
   Finest bread I will provide
   Till their hearts are satisfied.
   I will give My life to them.
   Whom shall I send?

Holy Ground

Words and Music by Geron Davis

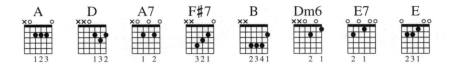

Strum Pattern: 1, 3
Pick Pattern: 2, 4

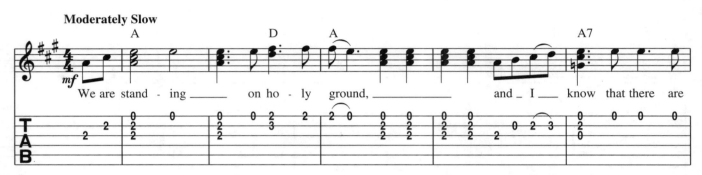

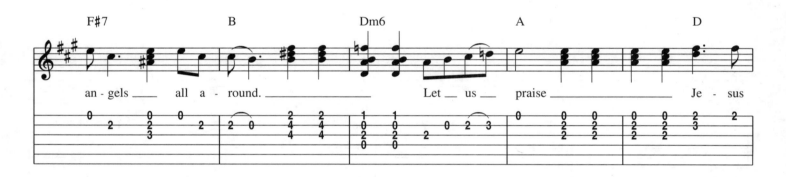

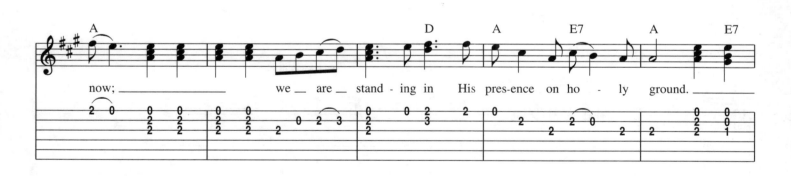

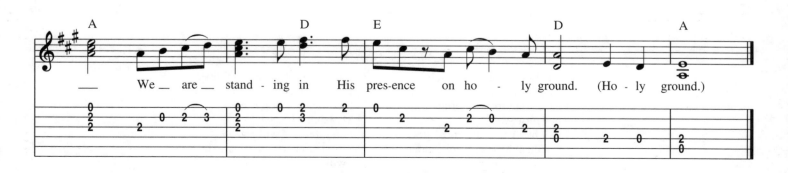

How Excellent Is Thy Name

Words and Music by Dick Tunney, Melodie Tunney
and Paul Smith

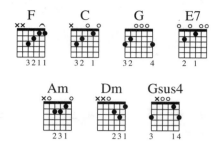

Strum Pattern: 1, 6
Pick Pattern: 3, 5

Verse
Moderately Slow

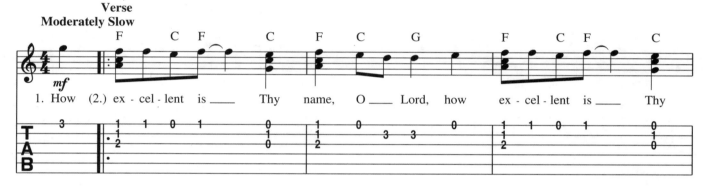

1. How (2.) ex - cel - lent is ____ Thy name, O ____ Lord, how ex - cel - lent is ____ Thy

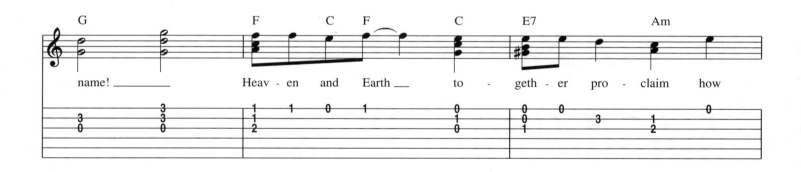

name! _____ Heav - en and Earth ____ to - geth - er pro - claim how

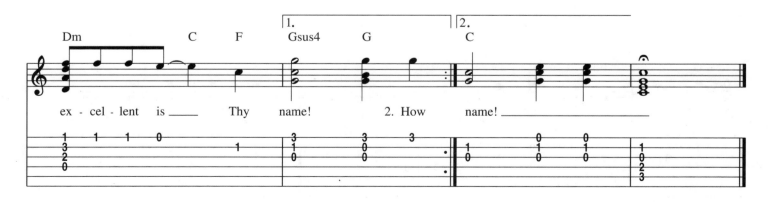

ex - cel - lent is ____ Thy name! 2. How name! _____

How Majestic Is Your Name

Words and Music by Michael W. Smith

I Love You Lord

Words and Music by Laurie Klein

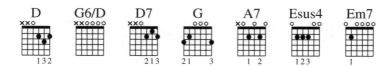

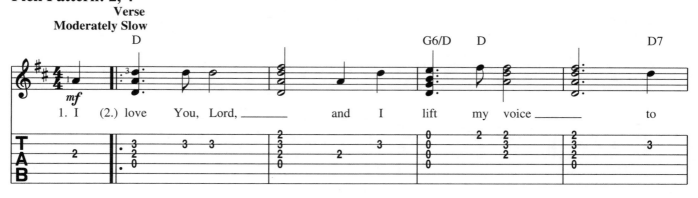

Strum Pattern: 1, 3
Pick Pattern: 2, 4

Verse
Moderately Slow

1. I (2.) love You, Lord, _____ and I lift my voice _____ to

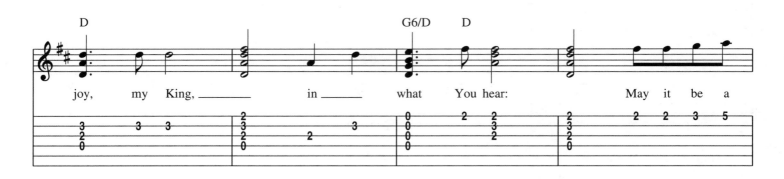

wor - ship You, O my soul, re - joice! Take

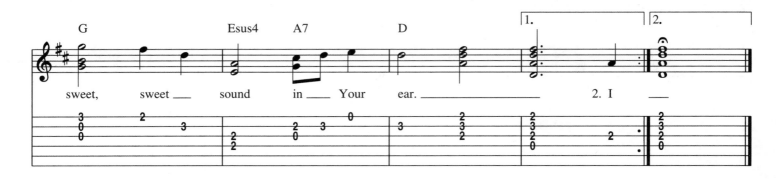

joy, my King, _____ in _____ what You hear: May it be a

sweet, sweet _____ sound in _____ Your ear. _____   2. I _____

I Love to Tell the Story

Words by A. Catherine Hankey
Music by William G. Fischer

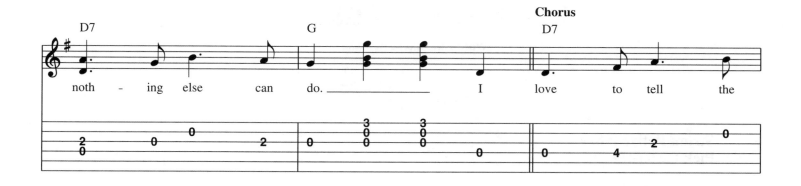

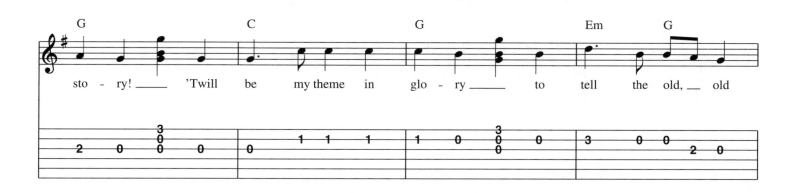

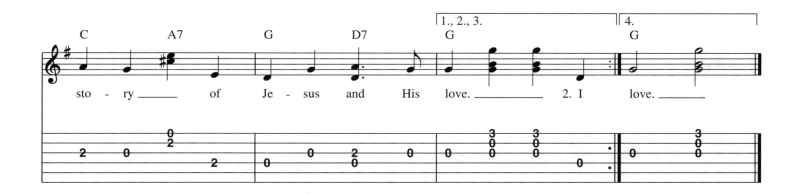

Additional Lyrics

2. I love to tell the story; more wonderful it seems
   Than all the golden fancies of all our golden dreams.
   I love to tell the story; it did so much for me,
   And that is just the reason I tell it now to thee.

3. I love to tell the story 'tis pleasant to repeat
   What seems each time I tell it, more wonderfully sweet.
   I love to tell the story for some have never heard
   The message of salvation from God's own holy word.

4. I love to tell the story; for those who know it best
   Seem hungering and thirsting to hear it like the rest.
   And when, in scenes of glory, I sing the new, new song,
   'Twill be the old, old story that I have loved so long.

Lamb of God

Words and Music by Twila Paris

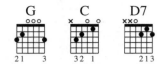

Strum Pattern: 8, 9
Pick Pattern: 8, 9

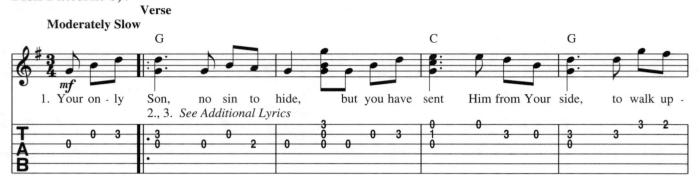

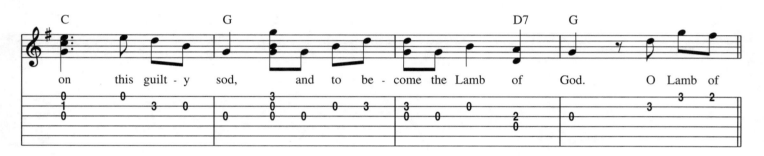

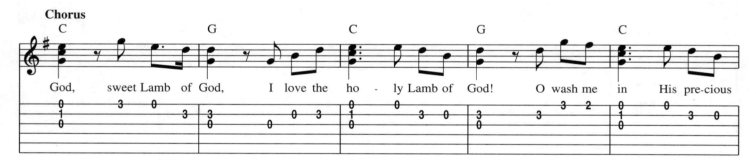

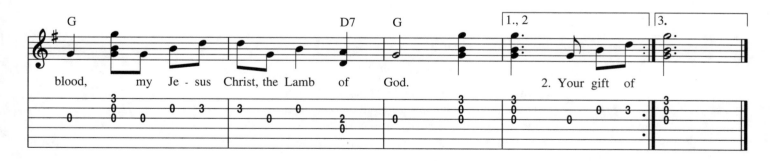

Additional Lyrics

2. Your gift of love, they crucified,
   They laughed and scorned Him as He died.
   The humble King they named a fraud
   And sacrificed the Lamb of God.

3. I was so lost, I should have died,
   But You have brought me to Your side,
   To be led by Your staff and rod,
   And to be called a Lamb of God.

Lord, Be Glorified

Words and Music by Bob Kilpatrick

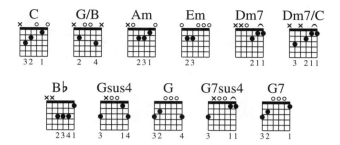

Strum Pattern: 3, 4
Pick Pattern: 3, 5

Verse
Moderately Slow

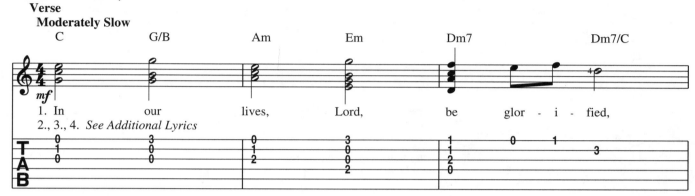

1. In our lives, Lord, be glor-i-fied,
2., 3., 4. *See Additional Lyrics*

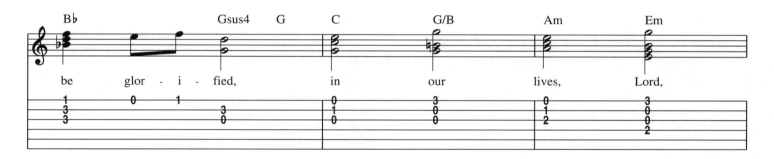

be glor-i-fied, in our lives, Lord,

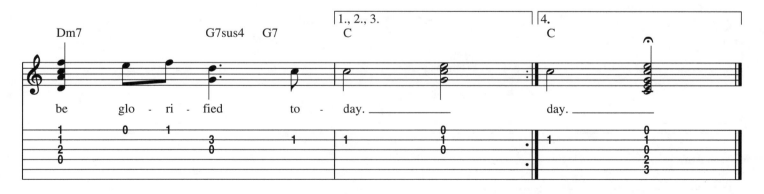

be glo-ri-fied to-day. ____ day. ____

Additional Lyrics

2. In our homes, Lord,
   Be glorified, be glorified,
   In our homes, Lord,
   Be glorified today.

3. In your church, Lord,
   Be glorified, be glorified,
   In your church, Lord,
   Be glorified today.

4. In your world, Lord,
   Be glorified, be glorified,
   In your world, Lord,
   Be glorified today.

Lord, I Lift Your Name on High

Words and Music by Rick Founds

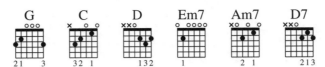

Strum Pattern: 1, 6
Pick Pattern: 2, 4

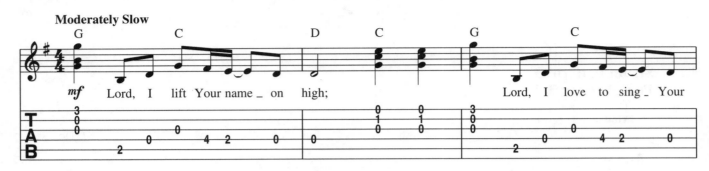

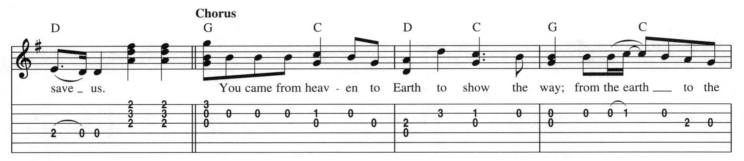

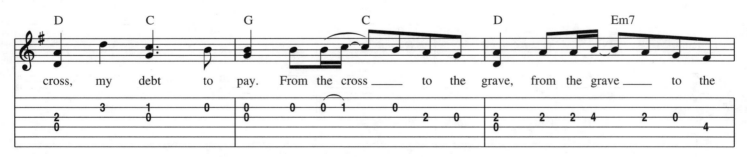

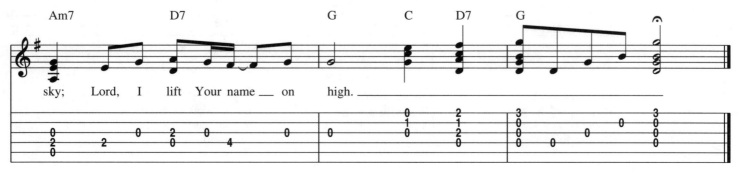

More Precious Than Silver

Words and Music by Lynn DeShazo

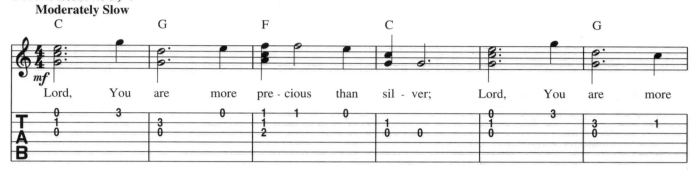

Strum Pattern: 1, 6
Pick Pattern: 3, 4

Moderately Slow

Lord, You are more pre-cious than sil-ver; Lord, You are more

cost-ly than gold. _____ Lord, You are _____ more beau-ti-ful _____ than

dia-monds and noth-ing I de-sire com-pares with You. _____

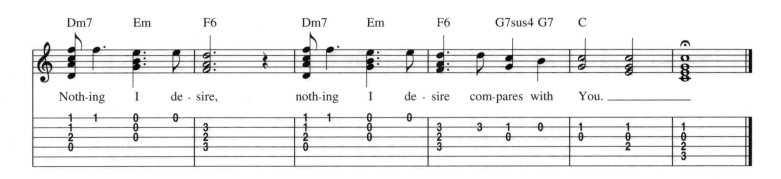

Noth-ing I de-sire, noth-ing I de-sire com-pares with You. _____

Majesty

Words and Music by Jack W. Hayford

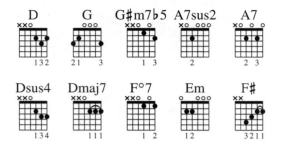

Strum Pattern: 3, 4
Pick Pattern: 4, 5

Verse
Moderately Slow

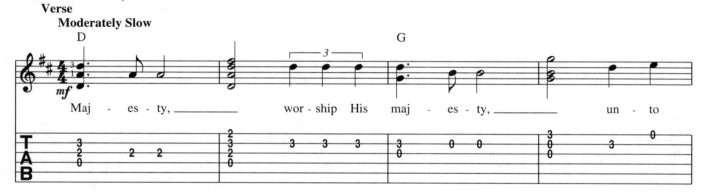

Maj - es - ty, _____ wor - ship His maj - es - ty, _____ un - to

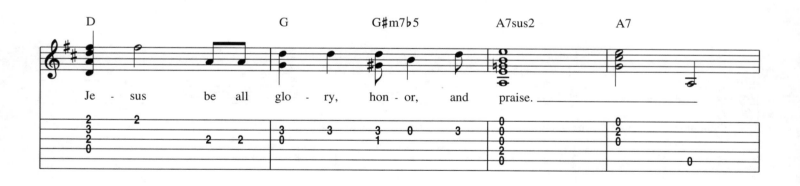

Je - sus be all glo - ry, hon - or, and praise. _____

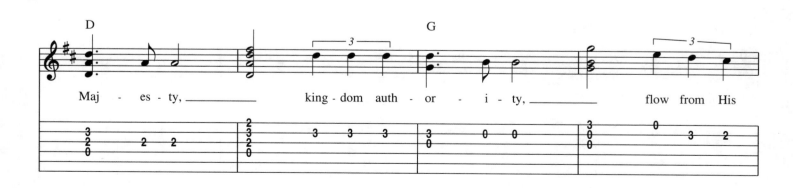

Maj - es - ty, _____ king - dom auth - or - i - ty, _____ flow from His

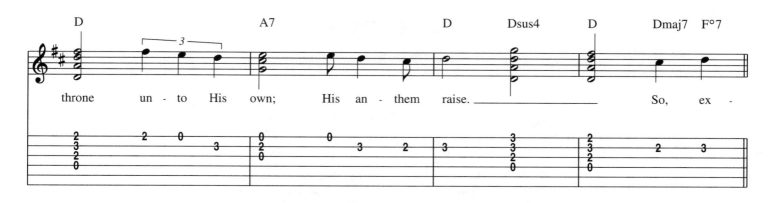

Chorus

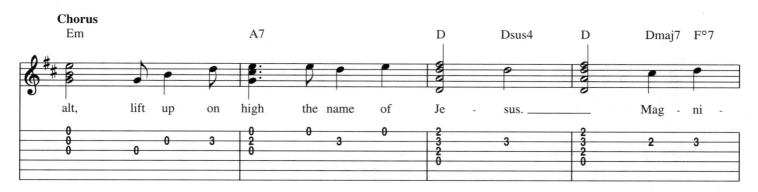

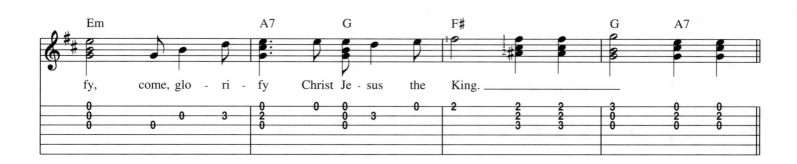

Outro

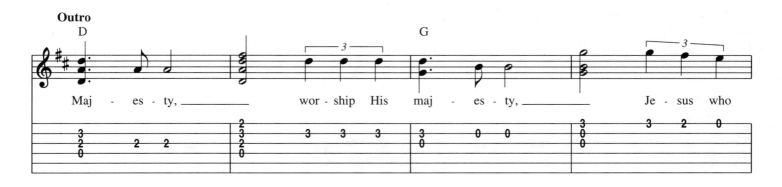

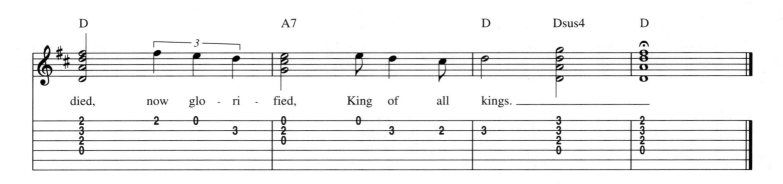

My Tribute

Words and Music by Andraé Crouch

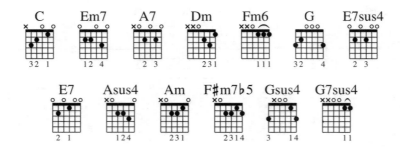

Strum Pattern: 1, 6
Pick Pattern: 2, 4

Verse
Moderately Slow

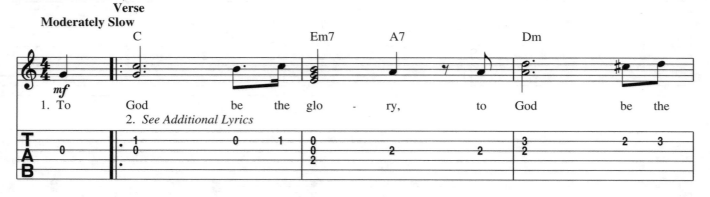

1. To God be the glo - ry, to God be the
2. *See Additional Lyrics*

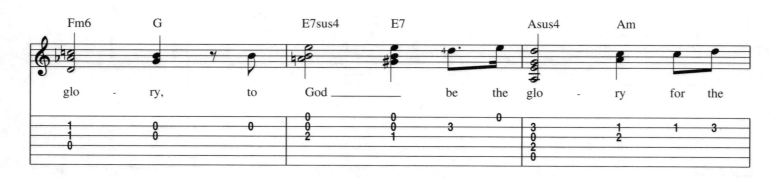

glo - ry, to God _____ be the glo - ry for the

things He has done. _____ 2. With His things He has done.

Additional Lyrics

2. With His blood He has saved me;
   With His pow'r He has raised me.
   To God be the glory for the things He has done.

O For a Thousand Tongues to Sing

Text by Charles Wesley
Music by Carl G. Glaser

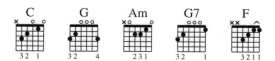

Strum Pattern: 8
Pick Pattern: 8

Verse
Moderately Slow

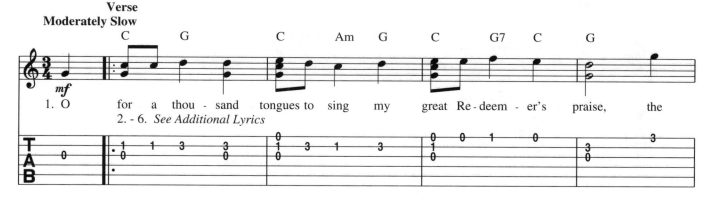

1. O for a thou - sand tongues to sing my great Re - deem - er's praise, the
2. - 6. *See Additional Lyrics*

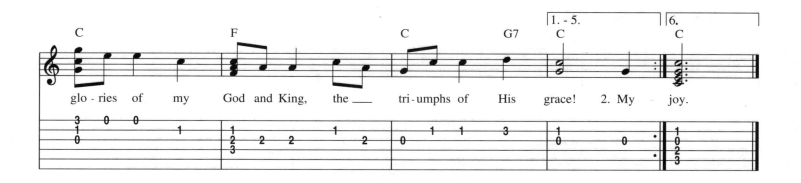

glo - ries of my God and King, the __ tri - umphs of His grace! 2. My joy.

Additional Lyrics

2. My gracious Master and my God,
   Assist me to proclaim,
   To spread through all the earth abroad,
   The honors of Thy name.

3. Jesus, the name that charms our fears,
   That bids our sorrows cease;
   'Tis music in the sinner's ears,
   'Tis life, and health, and peace.

4. He breaks the power of cancelled sin,
   He sets the prisoner free;
   His blood can make the foulest clean;
   His blood availed for me.

5. He speaks, and listening to His voice,
   New life the dead receive;
   The mournful, broken hearts rejoice,
   The humble poor believe.

6. Hear Him, ye deaf; His praise, ye dumb,
   Your loosened tongues employ;
   Ye blind, behold your Savior come,
   And leap, ye lame, for joy.

On Eagle's Wings

Words and Music by Michael Joncas

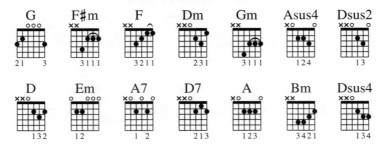

Strum Pattern: 4
Pick Pattern: 5

Verse
Moderately Slow

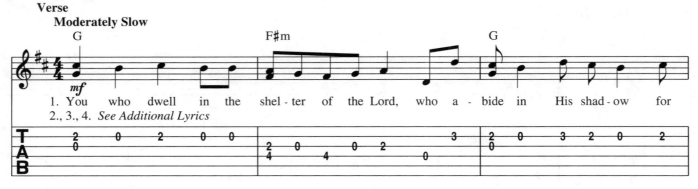

1. You who dwell in the shel-ter of the Lord, who a-bide in His shad-ow for
2., 3., 4. *See Additional Lyrics*

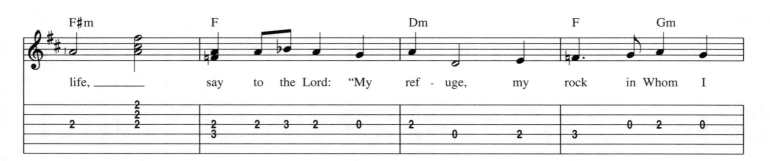

life, _____ say to the Lord: "My ref-uge, my rock in Whom I

Chorus

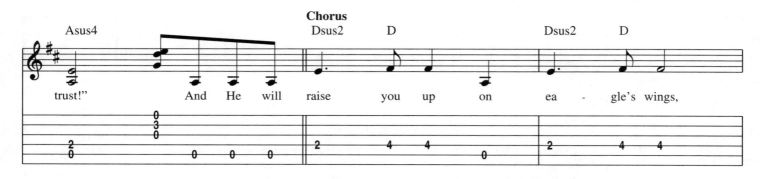

trust!" And He will raise you up on ea - gle's wings,

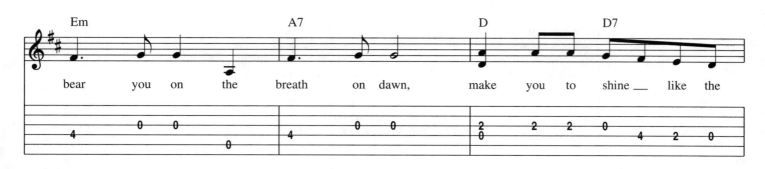

bear you on the breath on dawn, make you to shine ___ like the

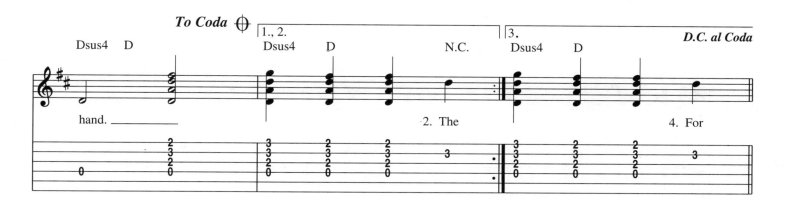

Coda

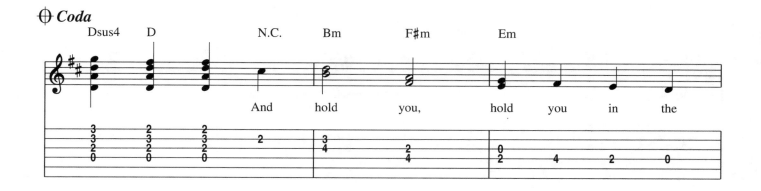

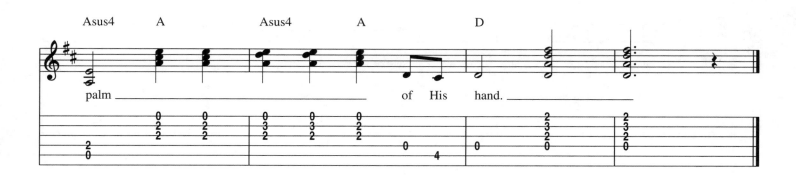

Additional Lyrics

2. The snare of the fowler will never capture you,
   And famine will bring you no fear:
   Under His wings your refuge,
   His faithfulness your shield.

3. You need not fear the terror of the night,
   Nor the arrow that flies by day;
   Though thousands fall about you,
   Near you it shall not come.

4. For to His angels He's given a command
   To guard you in all of your ways;
   Upon their hands they will bear you up,
   Lest you dash your foot against a stone.

Open Our Eyes

Words and Music by Bob Cull

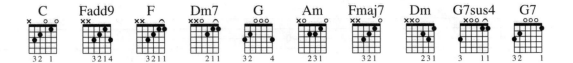

Strum Pattern: 7, 8
Pick Pattern: 7, 8

Verse
Moderately Slow

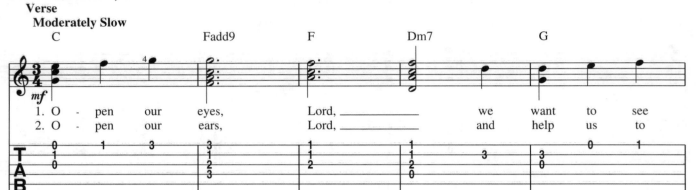

1. O - pen our eyes, Lord, _____ we want to see
2. O - pen our ears, Lord, _____ and help us to

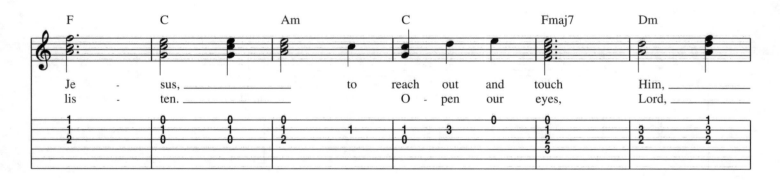

Je - sus, _____ to reach out and touch Him, _____
lis - ten. _____ O - pen our eyes, Lord, _____

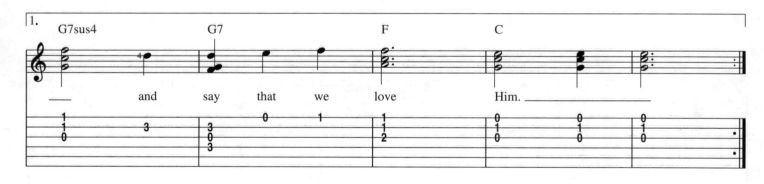

1.
___ and say that we love Him. _____

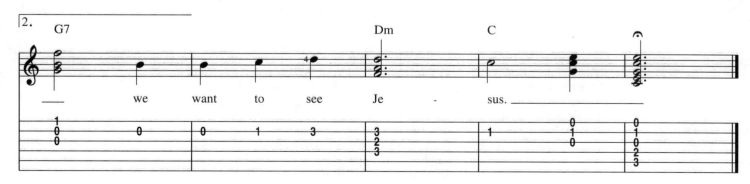

2.
___ we want to see Je - sus. _____

Praise the Name of Jesus

Words and Music by Roy Hicks, Jr.

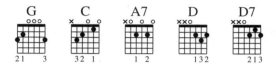

Strum Pattern: 3, 4
Pick Pattern: 1, 3

Moderately Slow

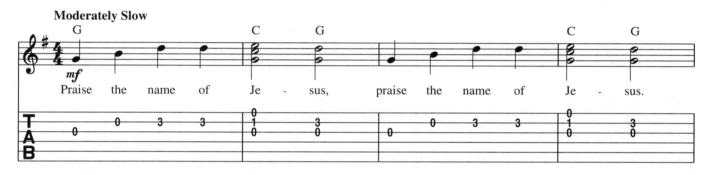

Praise the name of Je - sus, praise the name of Je - sus.

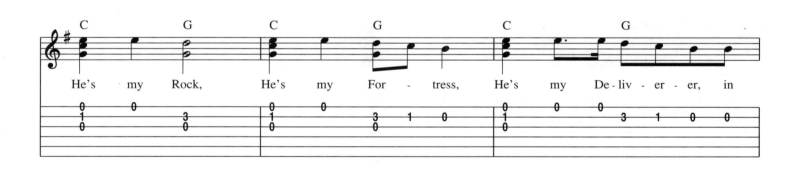

He's my Rock, He's my For - tress, He's my De - liv - er - er, in

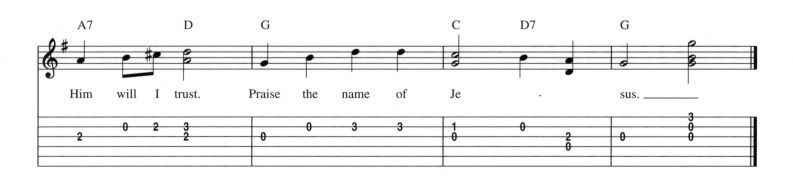

Him will I trust. Praise the name of Je - sus. _____

Seek Ye First

Words and Music by Karen Lafferty

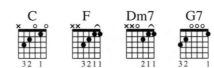

Strum Pattern: 4
Pick Pattern: 1

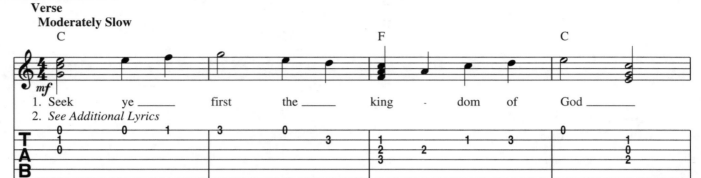

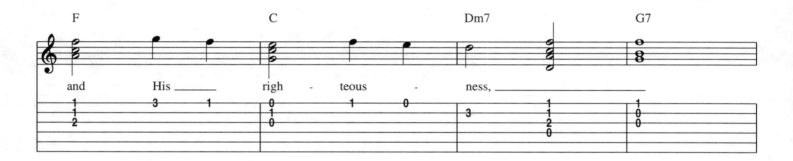

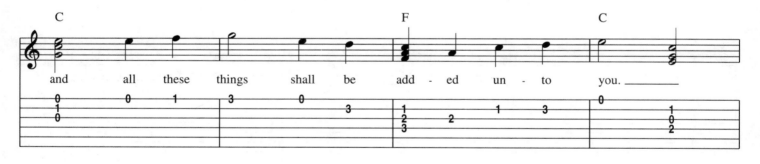

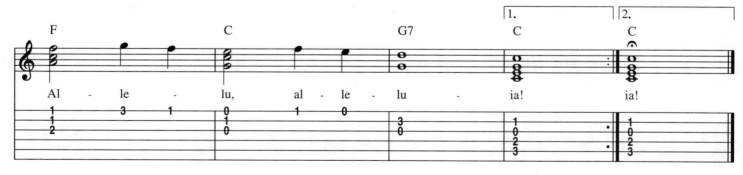

Additional Lyrics

2. Ask and it shall be given unto you,
   Seek and ye shall find.
   Knock and the door shall be opened unto you.
   Allelu, alleluia!

We Bring the Sacrifice of Praise

Words and Music by Kirk Dearman

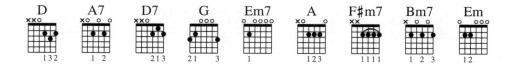

Strum Pattern: 1, 3
Pick Pattern: 2, 4

Verse
Moderately Slow

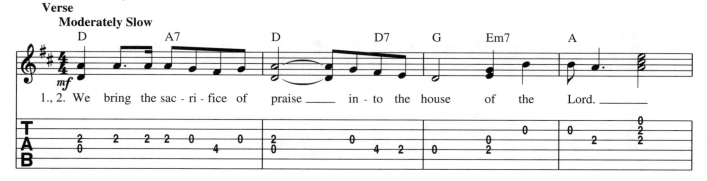

1., 2. We bring the sac-ri-fice of praise _____ in-to the house of the Lord. _____

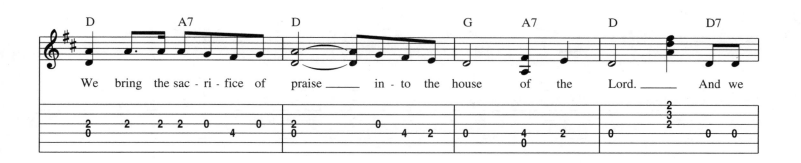

We bring the sac-ri-fice of praise _____ in-to the house of the Lord. _____ And we

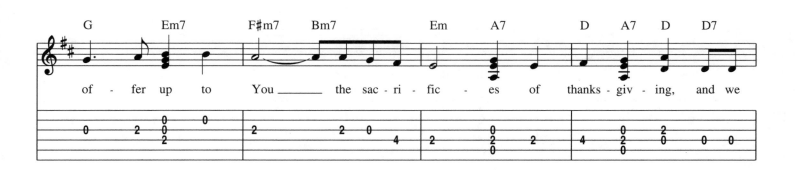

of-fer up to You _____ the sac-ri-fic - es of thanks-giv - ing, and we

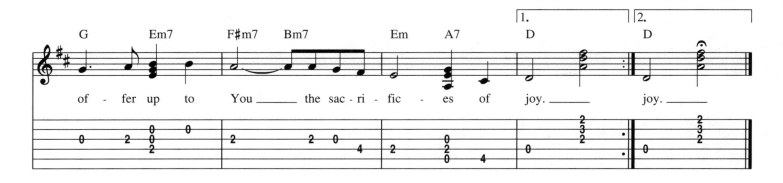

of-fer up to You _____ the sac-ri-fic - es of joy. _____ joy. _____

Shine, Jesus, Shine

Words and Music by Graham Kendrick

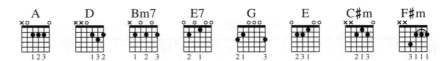

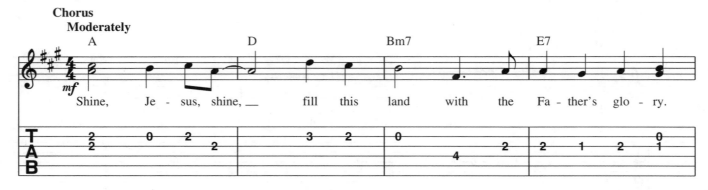

Strum Pattern: 6
Pick Pattern: 6

Chorus
Moderately

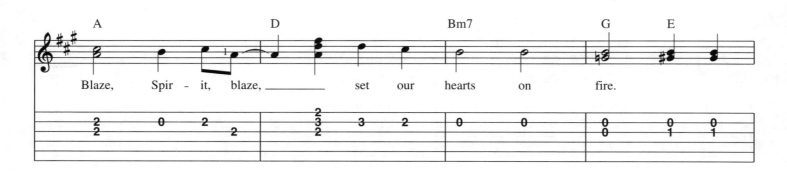

Shine, Je - sus, shine, ___ fill this land with the Fa - ther's glo - ry.

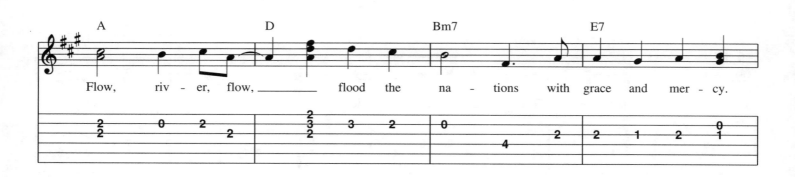

Blaze, Spir - it, blaze, ___ set our hearts on fire.

Flow, riv - er, flow, ___ flood the na - tions with grace and mer - cy.

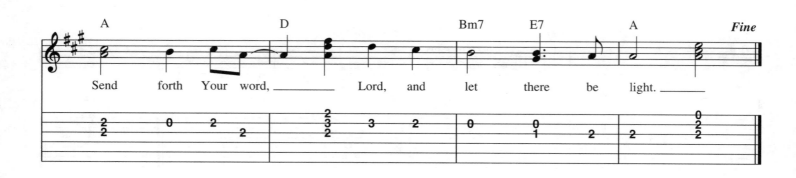

Send forth Your word, ___ Lord, and let there be light. ___

Fine

Verse

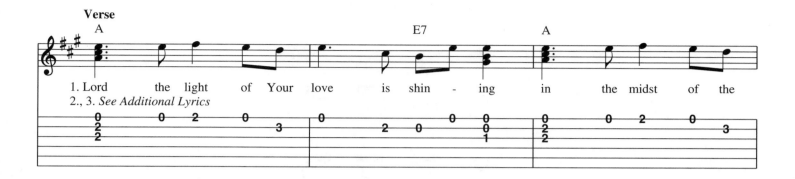

1. Lord the light of Your love is shin - ing in the midst of the
2., 3. *See Additional Lyrics*

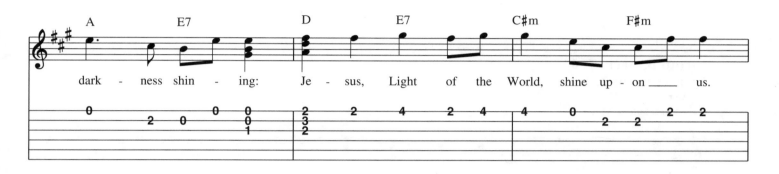

dark - ness shin - ing: Je - sus, Light of the World, shine up - on ____ us.

set us free by the truth You now bring __ us. Shine on ____

1., 2., 3.

3rd time, D.C. al Fine

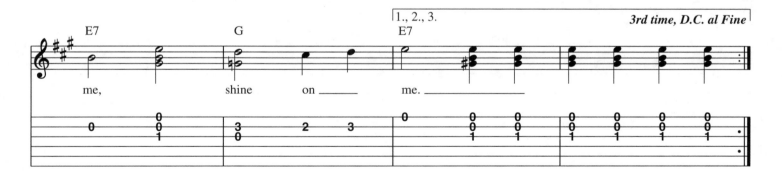

me, shine on ____ me. _____

Additional Lyrics

2. Lord, I come to Your awesome presence
   From the shadows in Your radiance;
   By the blood I may enter Your brightness,
   Search me, try me, consume all my darkness.
   Shine on me, shine on me.

3. As we gaze on Your kingly brightness,
   So our faces display Your likeness;
   Ever changing from glory to glory,
   Mirrored here may our lives tell Your story.
   Shine on me, shine on me.

Soon and Very Soon

Words and Music by Andraé Crouch

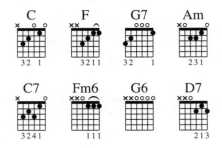

Strum Pattern: 1, 6
Pick Pattern: 2, 4

Verse
Moderately Slow

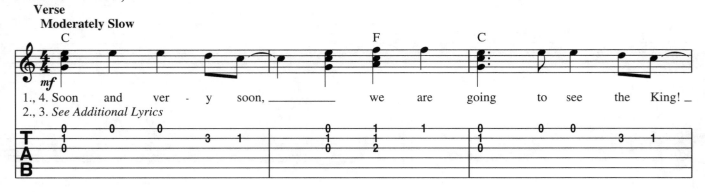

1., 4. Soon and ver - y soon, _____ we are going to see the King! _
2., 3. *See Additional Lyrics*

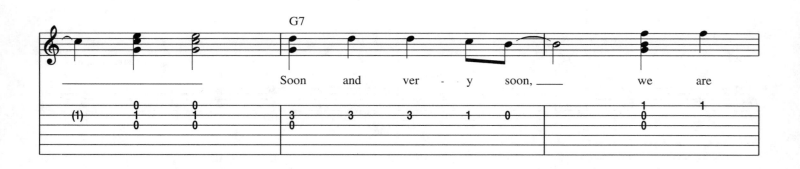

_____ Soon and ver - y soon, ___ we are

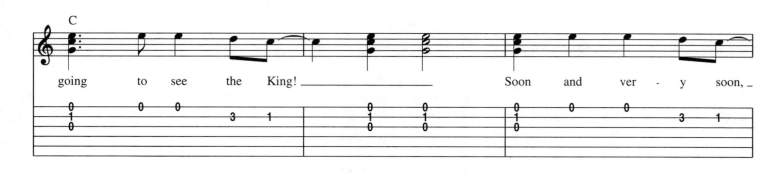

going to see the King! _____ Soon and ver - y soon, _

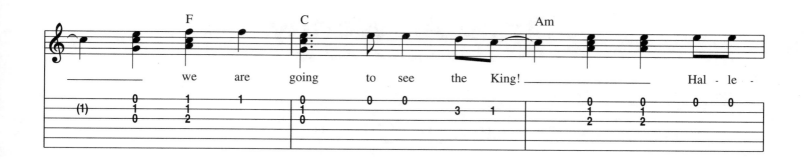

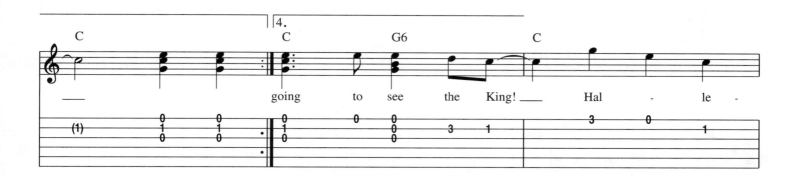

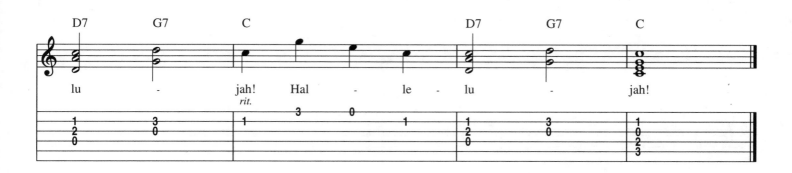

Additional Lyrics

2. No more crying there, we are going to see the King!
No more crying there, we are going to see the King!
No more crying there, we are going to see the King!
Hallelujah! Hallelujah! We're going to see the King!

3. No more dying there, we are going to see the King!
No more dying there, we are going to see the King!
No more dying there, we are going to see the King!
Hallelujah! Hallelujah! We're going to see the King!

Thou Art Worthy

Words and Music by Pauline Michael Mills

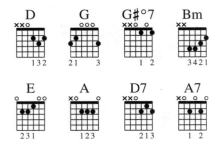

Strum Pattern: 8, 9
Pick Pattern: 8, 9

Moderately Fast

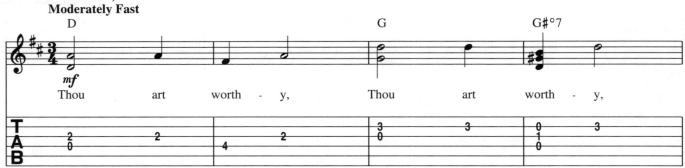

Thou art worth - y, Thou art worth - y,

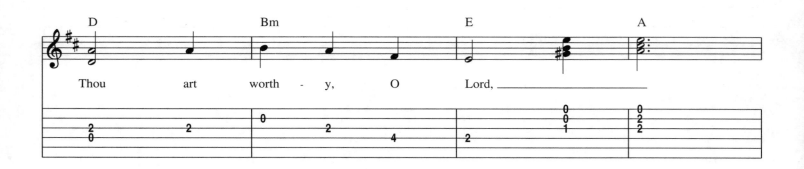

Thou art worth - y, O Lord, _____

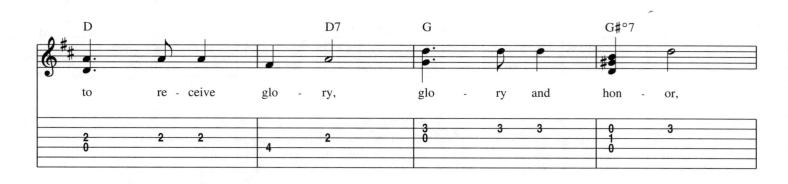

to re - ceive glo - ry, glo - ry and hon - or,

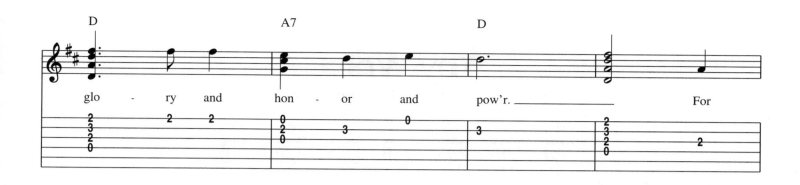

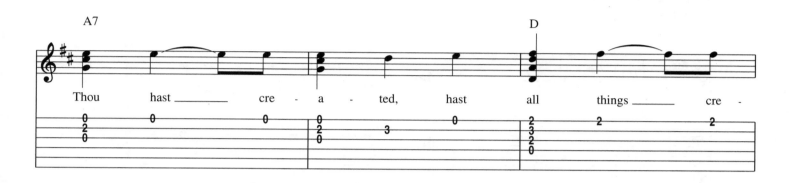

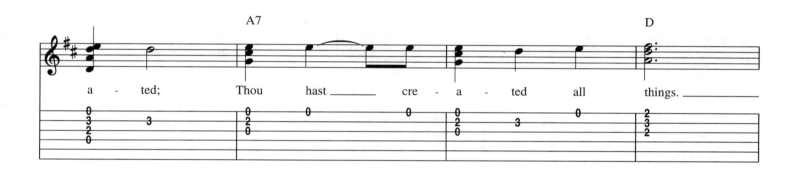

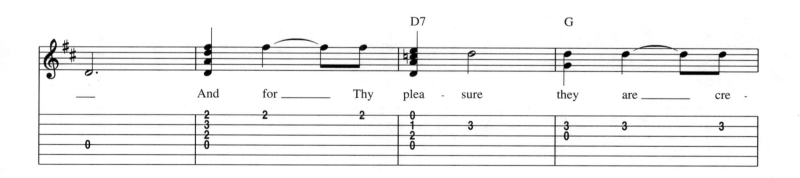

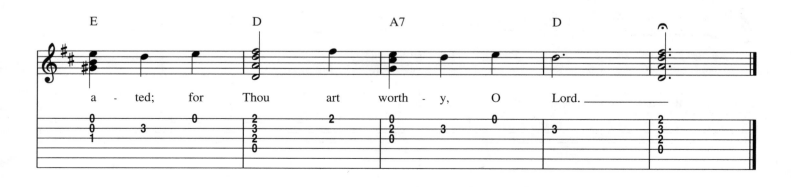

Thy Word

Words and Music by Michael W. Smith and Amy Grant

Strum Pattern: 1, 2
Pick Pattern: 2, 4

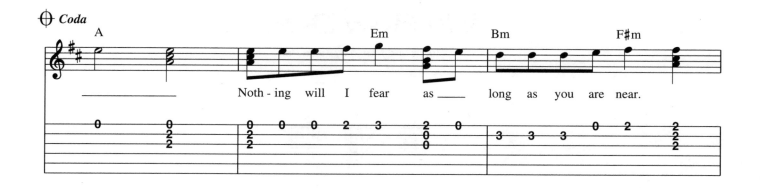

Coda

Noth - ing will I fear as _____ long as you are near.

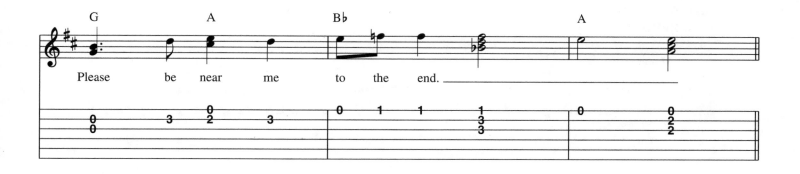

Please be near me to the end. _____

Chorus

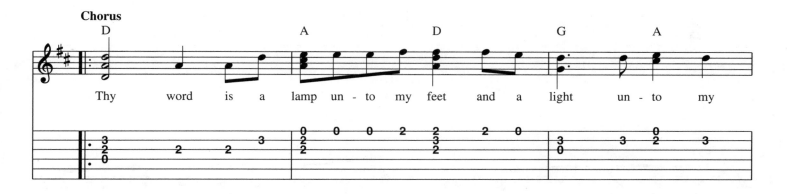

Thy word is a lamp un - to my feet and a light un - to my

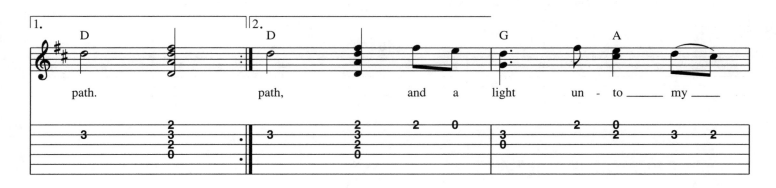

1.
path.
2.
path, and a light un - to _____ my _____

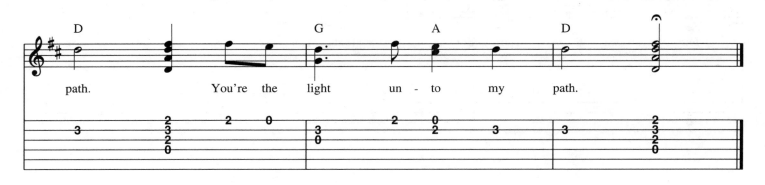

path. You're the light un - to my path.

We Bow Down

Words and Music by Twila Paris

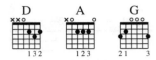

Strum Pattern: 8
Pick Pattern: 8

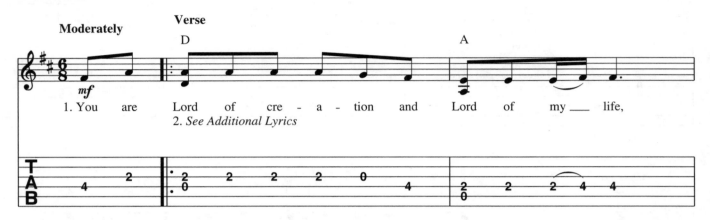

1. You are Lord of cre-a-tion and Lord of my ___ life,
2. *See Additional Lyrics*

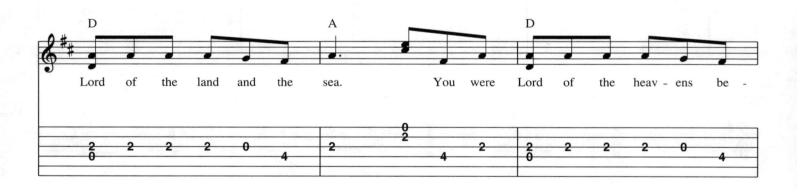

Lord of the land and the sea. You were Lord of the heav-ens be-

fore there was time, and Lord of all lords You will be. We bow

Chorus

down _____ and we wor - ship You, Lord. We bow down _____ and we
See Additional Lyrics

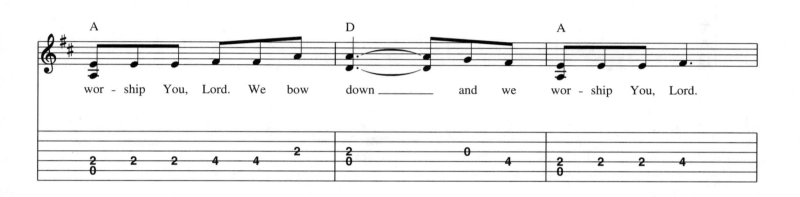

wor - ship You, Lord. We bow down _____ and we wor - ship You, Lord.

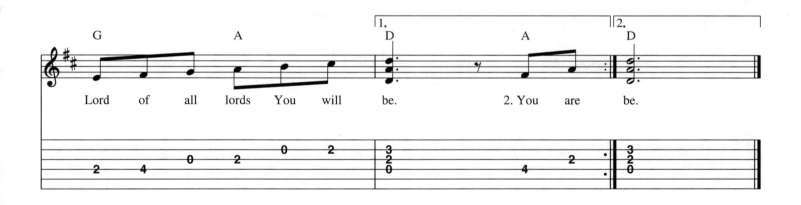

Lord of all lords You will be. 2. You are be.

Additional Lyrics

2. You are King of creation and King of my life,
   King of the land and the sea.
   You were King of the heavens before there was time,
   And King of all kings You will be.

Chorus We bow down and crown You the King.
         We bow down and crown You the King.
         We bow down and crown You the King.
         King of all kings you will be.

We Declare Your Majesty

Words and Music by Malcolm du Plessis

Strum Pattern: 1, 3
Pick Pattern: 3, 4
Moderately Slow

We Worship and Adore You

Traditional

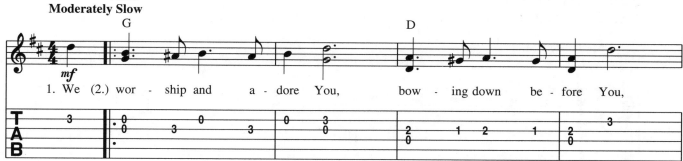

Strum Pattern: 3, 4
Pick Pattern: 1, 3

Verse
Moderately Slow

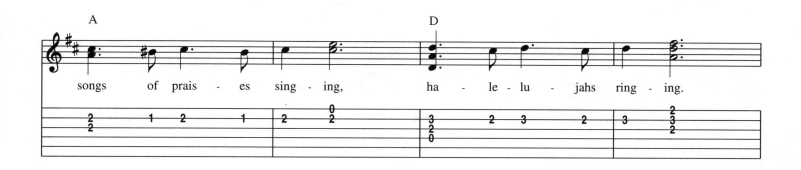

1. We (2.) wor - ship and a - dore You, bow - ing down be - fore You,

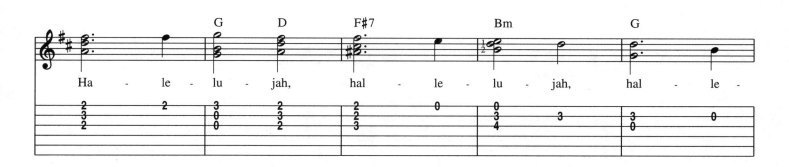

songs of prais - es sing - ing, ha - le - lu - jahs ring - ing.

Ha - le - lu - jah, hal - le - lu - jah, hal - le -

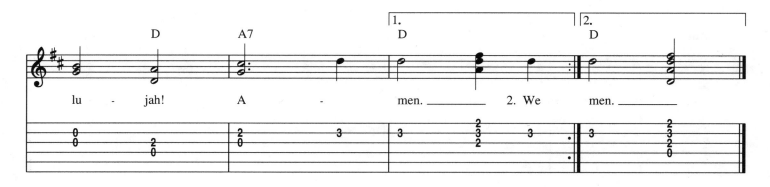

lu - jah! A - men. 2. We men.

You Are My Hiding Place

Words and Music by Michael Ledner

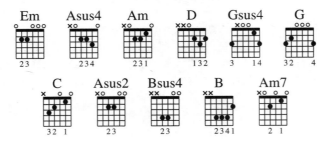

Strum Pattern: 1, 3
Pick Pattern: 2, 4

Verse
Moderately Slow

1., 2. You are my hid-ing place, You al-ways fill my heart with

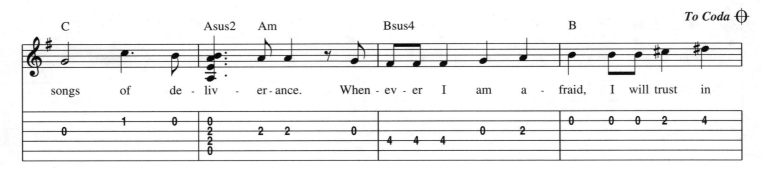

songs of de-liv-er-ance. When-ev-er I am a-fraid, I will trust in

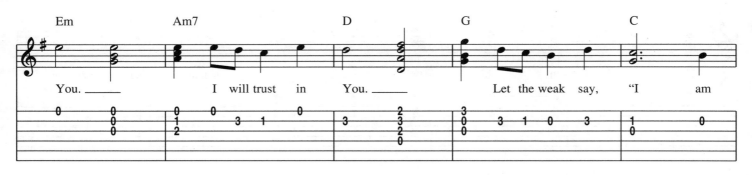

You. _____ I will trust in You. _____ Let the weak say, "I am

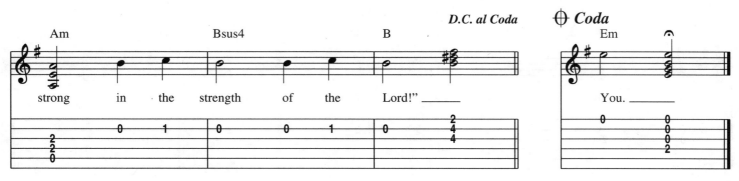

strong in the strength of the Lord!" _____ You. _____